T.F. RIGELHOF

NOTHING SACRED

A Journey Beyond Belief

GOOSE LANE

John Newlove's poem "The Double-Headed Snake" is reprinted from *Apology for Absence:
Selected Poems 1962–1992* and appears with the permission of Porcupine's Quill.

Edited by Laurel Boone.
Cover photographs: *Silver Maples,* © Roger J. Smith, 2003;
Interior of Reims Cathedral (detail), Philippe Colombi, Getty Images.
Cover and interior design by Julie Scriver.
Printed in Canada by Transcontinental.
10 9 8 7 6 5 4 3 2 I

National Library of Canada Cataloguing in Publication

Rigelhof, T.F.
Nothing sacred: a journey beyond belief / T.F. Rigelhof.

Incorporates A blue boy in a black dress, previously published separately, 1995.
ISBN 0-86492-382-I
I. Rigelhof, T. F. – Religion.
2. Authors, Canadian (English) – 20th century – Religious life. I. Title.

PS8585.I419Z472 2004   C813'.54   C2004-900149-3

Published with the financial support of the Canada Council for the Arts, the Government
of Canada through the Book Publishing Industry Development Program, and the New
Brunswick Culture and Sports Secretariat.

Goose Lane Editions
469 King Street
Fredericton, New Brunswick
CANADA E3B IE5
www.gooselane.com

For Ann, as always,
and for Roman, Alan,
Martin, and Paul.

CONTENTS

Introduction 9

ONE: *A River I Could Not Skate On* 17

TWO: *On My Knees* 27

THREE: *An Island of Treasures* 35

FOUR: *A New Year in Saskatchewan* 41

FIVE: *Glory Days* 51

SIX: *The Making of a Paper Boy* 61

SEVEN: *In the Middle of a Heartache* 75

EIGHT: *Saturday's Child* 85

NINE: *Thomas Merton and Me* 95

TEN: *403 Clarence Avenue North* 105

ELEVEN: *1963 and Dr. B.* 117

TWELVE: *Undoubtedly Thomist* 131

THIRTEEN: *Main Street, Ottawa* 143

FOURTEEN: *Kitchen Tales*   157

FIFTEEN: *History and Hysteria*   169

SIXTEEN: *You Can Call Me Al*   181

SEVENTEEN: *Catching Fire*   195

EIGHTEEN: *City of Churches*   207

NINETEEN: *Testament*   217

TWENTY: *Anger Management*   225

Epilogue   233

INTRODUCTION

On the morning of Tuesday, October 4, 1994, at about eight-thirty, a minor fire broke out in a chalet in Morin Heights, a small community in the Laurentian region of Quebec — a ski and summer resort and retirement area about an hour's drive north of Westmount on the island of Montreal, where I live. The first account I heard of the fire was on the five o'clock radio news, while I was washing salad vegetables at my kitchen sink. The report was fragmentary but said that two charred bodies had been found inside the chalet, that the chalet and a neighbouring one had been booby-trapped with timers and detonators attached to plastic containers of gasoline, that the chalets belonged to members of a cult called the Order of the Solar Temple, that there might be some connection to two other fires set at nearly the same time on Solar Temple properties in Switzerland, and that a massive international police investigation was under way. My immediate reaction was shallow and callous: I heard myself say, Shit, there goes a year's work.

I should have felt something deeper, but at least my reaction wasn't sentimentality or routine media-induced horror. At least I was feeling something personal.

The year's work was a satirical novel I'd convinced myself I'd almost finished writing, published later as *Badass on a Softail*. Until that October afternoon in 1994, my second published novel had a comic subplot featuring a religious organization modelled on the Solar Temple. In 1993, Grand Master Luc Jouret and two other Temple members had been arrested, charged with, and found guilty of attempting to purchase silencer-equipped revolvers. They were let off with thousand-dollar fines, but the matter did not end there. Several members resigned from the cult, and a handful took their stories to the media, which paid slight attention. It was summertime, and most reporters and readers were interested in other things. What attracted my eye was the clumsiness of a putative Master of the Universe, who allegedly knew the secret whereabouts of the Holy Grail among other great mysteries, but who was so naive and inept that he couldn't buy an illegal handgun in Montreal without getting caught. Any two-bit hood or even, come to that, anybody who isn't obviously a cop can find any shooter he wants if he's got cash in his pocket and knows how to have a quiet conversation in a bar with the guys at the back table. Jouret did not seem to lack money. This nicely fanciful combination seemed ripe for farcical treatment, especially after I'd been told by the guy behind the counter at a local sandwicherie, who'd been told by cops, that Luc Jouret had told the arresting officers that the guns were to be used to kill wild rabbits trespassing on the cult's organic gardens. The silencers would preserve the peacefulness of the neighbourhood.

In the following days and weeks, I learned what I could of the group as the facts gathered by the police fell into place. Cumulatively, the evidence suggested that the two leaders, Luc Jouret and Joseph Di Mambro, and at least twenty-eight other members of the Order of the Solar Temple believed themselves to be reincarnated elders of an ancient sect called the Rose and the Cross. The fatal fires were deliberately set as a purifying ritual through which the Elders of the Solar Temple expected to return to the Grand White Lodge of Sirius.

Before leaving this earth, however, twenty other people connected to them were shot in the head and their corpses were set on fire. A decade and several investigative reports later, it's still not clear whether many of these people were executed as enemies or simply assisted into outer space by their less fearful companions. It is clear that the two adults and the infant found dead in one of the chalets in Morin Heights — Antonio Dutoit, Nicky Robinson, and their infant son, Christopher Emmanuel — were regarded as serious threats to the cult. Di Mambro is said to have believed this child was the Antichrist.

In the midst of these revelations, Mark Abley phoned. A poet who wrote highly detailed and carefully constructed feature stories for the *Montreal Gazette* for many years, Mark knew me not only as a fiction writer but also as a book reviewer with a wide-ranging interest in religions of every sort. He wanted to know my opinion on why seemingly secure middle-class Quebeckers of Catholic background would so slavishly follow Luc Jouret to their deaths. This is what I told him: Jouret's group had a special emphasis on healing, both spiritual and physical. That healing seems to have been connected to astrology; to cleanliness of living, especially a proper diet; and to the body being seen as a special vessel, with an inner beauty of its own. People who join a group like this often come with particular ideas about their own health and the health of the world. And they find a home they can't find in mainstream society. Part of Jouret's dark power might have been his intuitive ability to win the devotion of such people. He might have told them, in effect, I realize how badly misunderstood you are — even by your own family. I can see that you have special insights. Mark and I talked for almost an hour, and I had more to say, especially about the group's Catholic and theosophical connections, but this is what the *Gazette* had space to print. I was satisfied with what I'd said, except for one thing: I'd spoken of Jouret's dark power without making it clear that its darkness came from the use Jouret made of it and not from any hellish point of origin. Far too much attention is given in the media to the magnetism of cult leaders, with their micro-empires of evil, and far too little to the longings, aches, hungers, and other appetites for love, comfort, and companionship of ordinary cult members. As far as one can see from the available video footage or make out from the reports of bystanders, Jouret wasn't unusually dynamic or self-confident, merely a good salesman with a peculiar pitch.

Then, media attention having moved on to the next important thing — would there or would there not be a hockey season? — I began to reflect on what a long, strange trip it is for anyone to shake loose from so comprehensive a world as Catholicism. I'd been there, I'd done that, I'd bought the T-shirt: six stiff white clerical collars, two black suits, and a couple of the long black dresses called soutanes or cassocks. I hadn't killed anyone in the name of my religion, but I'd tried to kill myself, and another seminarian had tried to murder me. Maybe that's too melodramatic: the attempted murder simply took my breath away, and the suicide fell a few feet short of fatal. Even so, they were signs of something larger and more significant that I'd never thought about as long and as hard as I ought to have done. At that point, I supposed I had the subject of another novel at hand — the autobiographical first novel that I'd never bothered to write. A few days later, while I was making notes for that serio-comic novel about my Catholic self, a second phone call came — this one from the poet, novelist, journalist, and sometime broadcaster David Helwig. David asked if I would write a book-length personal essay for an occasional series he was editing for Oberon Press in which creative people reflected on what they were doing and thinking twenty-five or thirty years earlier and how that was reflected in the lives they were now living. His proposal attracted me. I'd never written in an openly personal way in my fiction or anywhere else since I stopped writing poetry in my twenties. I thought it might be a nice warm-up to the novel I then supposed I was going to write as soon as I'd rewritten the parts of *Badass on a Softail* that required a greater distance from the realities of the Solar Temple. David thought the memoir was something I could draft and revise and he could edit in six months or less, since he wanted a slim book that might be easily read by an average reader in the course of an evening — thirty thousand words or so. I persuaded myself that the result would be of sufficient interest to some of my family, a few of my friends, and a couple of hundred ex-seminarians and ex-priests to be worth writing.

A Blue Boy in a Black Dress, published by Oberon in November 1995, exceeded my expectations by a long chalk. Reviewing it in the *Globe and Mail*, Hugo Meynall, a professor of religious studies at the University of Calgary, concluded a detailed and positive analysis of my book with these words:

> All in all, this is an amazing book, shrewd, sensitive and beautifully written. I hope that it will be widely read by those who wonder what the religious future will bring. One may perhaps still hold, in spite of the author, that there is something worth retaining under all the mal-practice, hypocrisy and power-mongering which continue to disfigure the Roman Catholic Church, but to go on believing so certainly requires the theological virtues of faith, hope and charity.

Much to my own amazement, Professor Meynall's view was shared by enough other readers that my little book has become my largest claim to fame as a writer. It was shortlisted for the Governor General's Literary Award for Non-Fiction (a prize won by John Ralston Saul's easily comprehended and urgent *The Unconscious Civilization*), and it won the QSPELL/Royal Bank of Canada Award. Much more importantly, it opened an always engaging and sometimes heated debate with a wider variety of readers than I'd ever expected to reach.

A Blue Boy in a Black Dress may or may not be the Canadian classic some people have said it is, but it is now very difficult to obtain and commands a substantial price on the rare book market whenever a copy in good condition becomes available. Most extant copies have passed through several readers and are dog-eared and heavily underlined. On occasion, I've even been asked to sign photocopies. When I undertook to prepare a new edition, I intended to write an introduction, update developments in world religions over the past decade, and revise my views wherever they'd altered. But events overtook me. I set to work in the closing weeks of December 2002, just as Cardinal Bernard Law resigned his post as head of the Boston archdiocese amid a flurry of news reports uncovering further sexual scandals in the Catholic Church, and I continued working through the war with Iraq and its aftermath. But between those events, on January 27, 2003, my life was interrupted and profoundly changed by a sudden hemorrhagic stroke that brought me nearer to death than I'd been since my seminary days. My stroke was a small one, a bruising on the left side of the brain that knocked out my right leg and foot for several weeks and caused collateral cerebral damage. Surprisingly, it also put me back in direct contact with parts of myself that I had pretty much forgotten. The upshot is *Nothing Sacred*, a book twice as long as *A Blue Boy in a Black Dress,* that retains only the parts, thoroughly re-edited, that time and circumstances have not altered. It reflects things that have claimed my attention during intervening years, and also, willy-nilly, it pays much more attention to the sexual lives of an officially celibate clergy than seemed important to me a decade ago. *A Blue Boy in a Black Dress* is where I was then; *Nothing Sacred* is where I am now but also contains much more of the child who is father to this man than the format of the earlier book permitted. Both start in the same place, but they diverge very quickly.

Not many hours before the fire that erupted in Morin Heights on the morning of Tuesday, October 4, 1993, Christopher Emmanuel Robinson Dutoit was stabbed through the heart more than once and a small wooden stake was inserted in his chest cavity because Joseph Di

Mambro believed this innocent infant was the Antichrist. This book is addressed to the innocence in all of us that is wounded every time anyone possessed by religion kills someone else anywhere for being what the murderer thinks he or she is rather than for anything the victim has done. Although all of us deserve flogging, as Shakespeare has it, none of us deserves to be put to death on the presupposition that what we are collectively — Jew, Muslim, Christian, Hindu, Buddhist, Marxist, Gypsy, gay — makes us individually worthy of execution.

In the face of that cold-blooded attitude to life, that widespread fiction which has hushed my own impulse to make stories up, I've come to believe that the only things that can save me from madness are keeping my attention focussed on details and remaining as reasonable as possible in the face of fear and regret, danger, and hardship. For me, being reasonable means accepting human diversity and embracing it in all its messiness. Those who follow ideologues, including the oligarch in the white dress and the triple crown, with his court in Rome, will find my reasoning profoundly disordered. You're forewarned.

"I have studied mankind and know my heart; I am not made like any one I have been acquainted with, perhaps like no one in existence," Jean-Jacques Rousseau writes at the beginning of his *Confessions* (1782), and he continues, "If not better, I at least claim originality, and whether Nature has acted rightly or wrongly in destroying the mold in which she cast me, can only be decided after I have been read." I make no such claim for myself. Nor do I claim, as he does, that my work "is without precedent." On the contrary, the longer I live, the more I'm struck by how common my experiences are and how representative they have been of the upwardly mobile sons and grandsons of immigrants who came of age outside the great cities of North America in the third quarter of the twentieth century. I think those parts of myself I write about may stand in for some readers and more of the people they want to read about — traditionally-raised men who knew the Second World War secondhand through the experiences of fathers and uncles, who were made uneasy by the American Dream of the fifties, rebelled in the sixties, and had difficulty coming to terms with increasing globalization ever since. All that is claimed for the "I" of this book is that he spent more time with books than most of his contemporaries and that he worked harder than many at disproving Schopenhauer's contention that "every man mistakes the limits of his vision for the limits of the world" by keeping his curiosity and imagination alive as best he could. I will say of what follows what Rousseau says of his work:

> I have concealed no crimes, added no virtues; and if I have sometimes introduced superfluous ornament, it was merely to occupy a void occasioned by defect of memory: I may have supposed that certain, which I only knew to be probable, but have never asserted as truth, a conscious falsehood. Such as I was, I have declared myself.

Westmount, Quebec, January 2004

ONE

A River I Could Not Skate On

When I decided to kill myself late in the winter of 1967, I wanted it to look like an accident. So no suicide note nor much mess. I was calm and level-headed about it. I wasn't angry at anybody. I spent a few minutes tidying up my room a little, just a little. No sudden departures, no quick changes. I left books and papers scattered every which way on my desk as they always were, as if I had every intention of returning, but I scooped up all the poems I'd been writing about death and stuffed them into an envelope, together with a few very personal souvenirs I didn't want the authorities to find and return to my family. I left my bank book and important personal papers in a clearly visible place, emptied the overflowing ashtray, and made my bed. Then I showered and shaved.

A guy who ran the folk and blues club in downtown Ottawa where I spent many of my Saturday nights called me "Bond," as in James Bond, more for my clothes than the body inside, and the nickname stuck with some of my friends. I had a closet full of fine clothes — perks from my summer job as a salesman in a department store. That day, I dressed in my favourite black suit which I'd had made to measure — a sharply pressed, very fashionable number, with a high three-button front,

17

narrow lapels, side vents, stovepipe trousers — a grey and white pin-stripe shirt, a black knit tie. I pulled on my ankle-high black suede Beatle boots: I could slide a mile on ice in them. In front of the full-length mirror on the inside of my closet door, I straightened my trouser legs, sleeves, shoulders, collar, and tie, and shot my cuffs. A bit bulky, a touch uncool. Underneath I was wearing thick winter under-wear that I normally wore only when I went skating, but there was a cold fog out, and I didn't want to be uncomfortable. Also, I figured it would weigh a ton when wet. I needed weight. I'd dropped to a hundred and twenty-eight pounds on a six-foot-tall, large-boned frame.

Tying a silk scarf loosely at my throat before pulling on my black cashmere overcoat, snap-brim fedora, and gloves, I left my room with the envelope under my arm. There was nobody in the corridors be-tween my room and the exit. I set off on the walk I'd been taking by myself every Thursday afternoon. Along the way, I carefully disposed of my poems and souvenirs in a refuse container at the construction site for the National Arts Centre.

I was two minutes early for my appointment, three minutes later than I usually was.

"How have things been this week?"

"I did what you suggested. I tried to visualize myself in twenty years."

"And what did you see?"

"I saw myself working in the country, half an hour outside Regina, at a place called Lumsden, Saskatchewan. I'm living there and teaching in the city, part-time, at the university. History is my subject. History of ideas. England in the eighteenth century. I've published my thesis and written a book, but I'm prouder of the poetry, even if people don't know it's mine because of the pseudonym. Three volumes, slim like everything from Faber and Faber."

"And what were you thinking about?"

"I had a big fire burning in the fireplace. I was watching the flames."

"Were you by yourself?"

"No, I had a dog with me."

"Were you depressed?"

"No, just regretful. You can't live without regrets, can you? I mean, people can't unless they're really vain, can they?"

"Why do you think that's the case?"

"They don't do enough, they do too much."

"What about you? What were you regretting?"

"Me? Missed opportunities — wife, kids, a better job, smarter books — the usual bullshit."

"Why do you call them that?"

I backed off into silence. The therapist was a nice guy. I knew he had a pregnant wife and probably dreamed of kids, pets, a tenured position, lots of published articles to his credit, a place in the country, dogs. I knew he was sensitive, not sensitive enough to write poetry like mine, but enough to feel he'd failed when he heard of my death. He'd know it wasn't altogether accidental. He was over thirty. Or seemed so. I was twenty-three.

"Tell me about the lake."

"Which lake?"

"The one outside your country place."

"There isn't one. The nearest lake to Lumsden is called Long Lake. It's the one my uncle drowned in, the one I told you about. That's the real resort area. Lumsden is just a small town in a valley with a river running through it. It has a ski hill."

"Oh, like the Laurentians. Where I come from."

"Don't think so. I've never gone skiing. I'm afraid of heights."

"But you're more afraid of water, aren't you?"

Deathly so, but that fear hadn't kept me from walking along Sussex Drive after my last few sessions with this psychologist at the university's health clinic and wandering into Rockcliffe and watching the ice crack and buckle on the Ottawa River with the slow coming of spring.

I'd picked out an accessible spot on the shore from which I could glide out on the ice and keep sliding in my Beatle boots until the ice gave way beneath me and the black waters swallowed me up. I had it all worked out, and it would have worked for me that Thursday except for the fog. Fog everywhere when I emerged from the clinic. Fog very thick in Major Hill Park, fog shrouding monuments, fog pinching my fingers and toes, fog in my eyes and throat and seeping into my brain, fog joining earth and sky. Fog up the river, fog down the river, fog inside my head. Should I do it? Could I do it? Couldn't I? Shouldn't I? Fog and more fog. Inside. Outside. And I still don't understand how it happened, but the river's edge was closer to me than expected and open with black water. There was no chance to glide and slide slowly over sheets of ice beyond the point of no return, and then there was the need to hurl myself downwards to meet death in a onrush of darkness. I screwed up courage to end my indecisiveness, fell forward before I was ready, and stopped short, held back at an odd, odd angle. Going nowhere, I began to laugh and cry and laugh.

"What did you think you were you doing down there? You could have been killed! Lucky for you I came along. That branch snagging your coat could have snapped at any time. Where did you say you live?"

"I think it was my foot caught between the rocks that really kept me from falling in. St. Paul's. On Main Street."

"You'd better get into the cruiser. I'll drive you home. I don't think I have to file a report, do I, Father? I guess God looks out for his priests, doesn't he?"

"Thanks. No, I don't think anybody has to be told about this."

I didn't tell the policeman he didn't have to call me Father. I didn't tell him I was two years short of being a priest. I didn't tell him that, as far as I knew, there wasn't any God looking out for me or for anybody else. If God existed, He was either asleep or missing in action. Me, I hadn't slept for many nights. Or days. I'd been studying God, and He'd kept slipping away from me until it seemed He was nowhere to be found.

A few days later I skittered away from St. Paul's, a seminary for out-of-town theology students at the University of Ottawa. During a break in classes at Easter, I went to stay with my older brother, who was completing a PhD in mathematics at McMaster University in Hamilton. While there, I made an appointment with E.P. Sanders, of the religion department. He offered me a place in the graduate program, with a fellowship attached, and an additional bursary, so that I could study Hinduism during summer school and advance my standing in the masters program by a year. George Grant was going to be on sabbatical, but I'd be able to study with him when he returned. I went back to St. Paul's a little less exhausted.

The following Thursday, I saw my therapist for the last time. I didn't tell him about my suicide attempt. I crammed and I crammed and attempted to write the final examination for a Baccalaureate in Sacred Theology, even though I was convinced that it was a subject without an object. I failed so miserably that my teachers were utterly astonished.

"Have you lost your faith?"

"I've not been sleeping well."

I went to bed and slept for twenty hours straight. When I woke up, I packed all my belongings, went home to my mother in Regina, and took a job in a dairy for a few weeks. On Saturday July 1, 1967, I was celebrating Canada's centennial on an eastbound train passing through Sudbury with a Toronto art student who showed me a letter Leonard Cohen had left under her pillow. Two days later, I started my life as a graduate student at McMaster by auditing a summer school course on Hindu philosophy. Within three months, I'd retaken my theology exams, been awarded my BTh, and met the love of my life. Within two years, I'd married, completed an MA with a thesis exposing a nineteenth-century historian's misreading of an eighteenth-century theologian's mistaken reading of scientific evidence in support of the reasonableness of Christianity, developed strong interests and some knowledge in Hinduism and Buddhism, and studied with George Grant while he was moving from his concern with *Technology and Empire* to his examination of Nietzsche in *Time as History*. I'd also completed my coursework for a PhD, published a few poems and reviews under my own name, and arrived in Halifax to take up a lecturer's position at St. Mary's University. Some Americans were preparing to put a man on the moon, others were planning Woodstock, and another half million of their countrymen were trying not to get killed in Vietnam while burning villages, shooting peasants, and randomly impregnating the female population. My wife and I moved to Montreal in the middle of the Watergate hearings, and I became a college teacher of religion and humanities, a novelist, and a short story writer. For many years, I refused to teach anything connected with theology or the Catholic Church. From time to time, I've suffered terrible bouts of depression resulting from biochemical and affective imbalances, but I've never again considered suicide as a realistic alternative: having survived the loss of my religion, I've been able to handle whatever else has come along without becoming violent.

I first told this story in *A Blue Boy in a Black Dress*, and readers still contact me. Mostly they want to tell me stories about their own experiences of growing up within strict religious environments, inside and outside Catholicism, but sometimes they have questions they want to ask, and for some time now, the questions keep coming back to one thing — sexual abuse. They've heard that the victims of sexual abuse have low self-esteem, are frequently suicidal. They want to know if I was sexually abused. They seem genuinely relieved to hear that I wasn't molested or raped, but almost disbelieving. Then they ask if I was aware of sexual abuse going on around me. That's not surprising, and the question requires some answer. It's not enough to say we were living in a more innocent time and leave it there.

"Pervert. Pedophile."

The speaker is an Irish Montrealer, a man in his late fifties, my age, standing behind me at my neighbourhood supermarket checkout. His face is flushed. His eyes are fierce. He motions his head towards the exit. The automatic doors are closing behind a priest.

"They should all be locked up. Throw away the keys. I told him that to his face. At the bakery counter."

I don't know which is more surprising, such sudden incivility stated so matter-of-factly or the sight of a priest in a public place in his black dress, his cassock, in 2002. Once familiar, men in clerical garb of any kind are rarely sighted here on the streets of Montreal in the new millennium. Outside the store, I see the priest sitting in the front passenger seat of an old van. As I catch sight of him handing his driver an orange from his plastic shopping bag, I think I recognize the face of a seminary classmate. But thirty-five years and much else separate us now. His face is distinct even under a beret and shaded by sunglasses, but I pass by and don't look back. If he is my old classmate, I can't remember his name or much else about him except that he played hockey and was surprisingly good at it. Players didn't wear helmets in those days, and he was the only one I ever saw wear a beret instead of a toque or earmuffs on the ice. He had a certain style. I remember that I liked him. And, then, that sometimes he listened to Bob Dylan records with me and my friends. And that sometimes I listened to Jacques Brel records with him and his friends. And that he smoked my Russian Sobranie cigarettes whenever I had any, and he always offered me Gauloises in return. Then, as I turn up the walk to my front door, I remember that we liked to tease one another.

I recall saying to him once, "You don't believe for a moment that Jacques Brel is alive and well and living in Paris. You think it's a case of mistaken identity. In fact, you're sure it's really God hiding out there on the Left Bank in a beret and dark glasses, playing guitar, singing 'La Mort.'"

That, like my failed suicide, was in 1967. At that time, a very clamorous minority of seminarians believed that if we were to seriously profess the Apostle's Creed and proclaim it to others, we had to know and be able to counter the most telling arguments against every single article of faith. Including the existence of God. We supported Vatican II wholeheartedly. Karl Rahner and Hans Küng, advisors to the German bishops, were our theological heroes. We might not have known what we were doing, but we were sure we knew what needed to be undone in a church that had failed the world and failed itself during World War II and the Cold War.

Now, it was Sunday morning, December 15, 2002, and I was sitting in my kitchen uncomfortably reading a two-page spread in the *Montreal Gazette*, "Catholic Church Caught in Turmoil." It was just the latest instalment in the continuing story of sexual crimes of clergy and cover-ups by their bishops. Two days earlier, Cardinal Bernard Law had resigned as Archbishop of Boston, and *Gazette* stories from Rome, London, and New York assessed his resignation and its consequences. The story from Rome reminded readers that "Cardinal Bernard Law . . . may have been the highest-ranking church official to fall in the ongoing sex-abuse scandal, but he wasn't the first." And then it provided a quick summation of "a worldwide problem," citing the resignations of Bishop Brendan Comiskey of Ferns, Ireland, for protecting an abuser, and Archbishop Juliusz Paetz, of Poznan, Poland, and Auxiliary Bishop Franziskus Eisenbach, of Mainz, Germany, accused of abusing others. In its final paragraph, the story noted other cases surfacing in Australia, Hong Kong, and South Africa. Another article said, "The Survivors Network of those Abused by Priests has named Cardinal Edward Egan of New York and Cardinal Roger Mahoney of Los Angeles as the next targets of its campaign. The network claims that both cardinals have been as negligent as Law." The authors pointed out that the Boston archdiocese "has already paid out tens of millions of dollars" and was trying to decide if it "should file for bankruptcy to deter further civil lawsuits"; the authors believed that a steep decline in donations from wealthy Boston congregations had finally led the papal curia to advise the Pope to accept Law's resignation, rather than the mountain of evidence that had been collected of "a devastating, powerful and disgusting cover-up of criminal conduct."

Criminal conduct? There's no question whatsoever in my own mind or in the minds of people who talk to me that non-consensual sex is a crime and that sex with a child is a matter for civil prosecution and severe punishment that fits the crime, not tempered to suit the criminal. But that isn't the curia's perspective. As the story from New York made clear, the Vatican had refused to accept the zero-tolerance sexual-abuse policy that American bishops had drafted because it felt "those bishops were letting external forces trump internal control," and it cast Law's resignation "less in terms of his failures than in terms of factors beyond his control." Vatican sources suggested that "the American news media had exaggerated the cardinal's errors and gone overboard in vilifying his actions." The story quoted an unnamed Vatican official as holding the view that "Law's mistakes were the result of a lack of knowledge about abusers" and that Law had to go only because he had lost the capacity to lead.

All this is old news now, replaced month by month by new revelations of the foul mess priests and bishops and cardinals and popes have made in their church. I took special note of it at the time because I was struck by the obvious irony that Cardinal Law hadn't lived up to his name. I didn't need to cast my mind back to the seminary courses I took on canon law to remind myself that there's a distinction between culpable and inculpable ignorance. All good citizens know that the people responsible for upholding laws must inform themselves of all things relevant to those laws, and that they are not just poorly informed and foolish but guilty of neglect of duty if they don't.

Bishops preside over ecclesiastical courts. They are required to have legal advisors.

The Vatican official's excuse is not only self-serving and fatuous, it also runs against the one thing that seemed fundamental of the Catholic Church of my childhood — it cared for children and put their welfare first. I tracked the details of this case partly because Cardinal Bernard Law has been one of the principal architects of the conservative revival: it was Law who proposed that the church issue the Catechism of Catholic Doctrine that has been used to drive out the kind of theological questioning seminarians of my generation engaged in. It was Law who made certain that the US Bishops Conference never issued its Pastoral Letter on Women. It was Law who described abortion as "the primordial evil of our day," preferring to focus on the destruction of potential children rather than on the ruination of living children.

TWO

On My Knees

When I was a schoolboy living at 209 Angus Crescent in Regina, Saskatchewan, in the fifties, my religion was Catholicism, and Catholicism was simply there. It was not the only religion. An erstwhile Baptist minister, Tommy Douglas, lived next door. Billy, my best friend, who lived two doors up, was an Anglican and the grandson of a Methodist circuit rider. The neighbours across the street were Lutherans. Pentecostals lived in one of the terraced houses at the end of the lane to Leopold Crescent. I sometimes played with two Jewish boys my own age, and a Christian Science lady often paid me to run errands. But Catholicism encompassed me, as natural a force as water, air, earth, and fire. It was tactile, sonorous, elemental, and by turns comforting and threatening. And it set me apart from non-Catholics: Catholics knew the world was going to end on January 1, 1960, or was it 1990? Pope Pius XII knew with absolute certainty the very hour to the precise minute because one of the three children to whom the Blessed Virgin Mary had appeared at Fatima — was it Lucy? — had written the Holy Father a letter telling him what Jesus' mother had told her. The Pope had fainted. The Pope was ours, and his knowledge was infallible, and we listened to him and said the extra prayers at the end of Mass so that

Russia would be converted. If we wanted to guarantee that every member in our own family would be together in heaven, we had to gather together on our knees and say the rosary every night after supper. So we did, and my father stuck what would now be called a bumper sticker in the shape of a scroll to our front door proclaiming, "The Family That Prays Together Stays Together." It was a badge announcing our faith to postmen, milkmen, bread men, and Fuller Brush salesmen. Our immediate neighbours needed no telling. Every Friday they could smell fish frying. Every Sunday morning they could see all of us turning out in our best clothes for Mass and Communion at Holy Rosary Cathedral, a twelve-minute walk from home for mother and sisters in high heels, a seven-minute trot for me on foot. Sunday breakfast wasn't a meal; it was a reward of pink grapefruit with half a red maraschino cherry in the middle and crisp bacon and fried eggs sunny-side-up and toast and strawberry jam. The reward was for fasting since midnight and staying pure and sinless at least since Confession on Saturday afternoon.

Few neighbours, even our fellow Catholics, rose early enough to see my father and me making that same journey to the cathedral on weekday mornings. I remember it best in autumn, my older brother already in high school and exempt, irritated by the ringing of the alarm at five forty-five but wakeful enough to push me out of bed. On cold, creaking floors, I tiptoe to the bathroom to splash sleep from my eyes with icy water and brush my teeth, taking care not to swallow water or Pepsodent toothpaste and inadvertently break my fast. Dressed, protected in my windbreaker against the pre-sunrise chill, I let myself out the front door and sit on the wooden railing of our veranda and breathe in the wonderful smell of fallen, rotting leaves and wait for my father to finish shaving. He joins me, morocco-bound Daily Missal in one hand, and we walk together, his other hand holding mine, scrunching leaves underfoot through a tunnel of bare trees, the deep blue sky pierced with pinpricks of starlight. That tunnel of silent communion between us winds through four blocks of city street and up the rectory driveway, which narrows to double body width at the side entrance of the cathedral. Inside the door, we separate. I'm to serve Mass.

I remove my shoes at the sacristy entrance, turn on the lights, and scurry across the red carpet in stocking feet. There's a walk-in closet in the sacristy. I hang up my windbreaker and find a pair of blue leather altar slippers in my size and a half-buttoned cassock, which I step inside and pull on and button to my throat. I slip a starched surplice that smells of ironing over my head and go to the mirror above the sink and flatten my hair with water on my comb. I fill one glass cruet with water from the sink and another with sacramental wine from the cupboard under the sink, using a glass chemist's funnel that has to be rinsed and turned upside down to dry. I arrange the cruets on a small tray with a starched linen towel and carry the tray to the table beside the altar. The sanctuary is dimly lit by a large candle that burns perpetually in a red glass candle holder. A second light, a reading lamp, casts a golden halo of light over the head of the priest reading his breviary in the altar stalls. This morning it's Father Walt, and I leave the sacristy carefully and double-check my appearance in the mirror. Father Walt is fussy. For him, everything must be perfect. I hold myself in readiness for inspection. When he's finished his prayers, he looks me over in the sacristy. After a tug or two at the neck of the surplice, I get the nod to go light the candles. The lighter is a long wooden-handled metal tube that holds a taper. I can't allow it to drip wax on the altar cloths, so I move with quick smooth gestures, easy when there are two candles to light, notoriously difficult when I have to stand on a step to reach the six larger ones for a High Mass. There are three Masses every morning at the cathedral, and it's not unusual for two of the three to be Requiem High Masses; the cathedral's large and prosperous congregation buys a lot of expensive Masses to commemorate their dead. Father Walt is the only one who likes singing this early in the morning, but today, to my relief, his Mass is a two-candle affair. Even so, as he faces the robing table, he warbles a few scales as he arranges the white linen amice on his shoulders and loops its two ribbons across his chest, behind his back and around his waist before tying their ends in a precisely centred perfect bow. The amice not only provides the right kind of neckline for the other vestments, it also protects them from perspiration stains and misadventures with hair creams. My father is a Brylcreem man and a little dab of that does him just fine. Father Walt uses something even less oily, with an odour completely unknown to me; he does not smell like any of the smells in the corner barbershop. He's the most exotically scented and fastidious man I've ever known. Then the long white linen gown called an alb, bunched together, kissed, over his head, smoothed down over the heavier cloth of his soutane. His one-size-fits-all alb is much too long for him. The braided cord of his cincture is looped around his waist, tied in its own special knot. Pulling the alb up and blousing it out over the cincture, he adjusts its length, straightens the hem, tightens the cincture. He loops the coloured silk stole around his neck, crosses it over his chest, holds the tasselled ends in place with loops of cincture. I pin the coloured silk ceremonial hand towel called a maniple to his sleeve. This is a tricky manoeuvre, and he doesn't let many boys attempt it. It is all too easy to stick him with the pin. Finally the outer garment, a silk chasuble with an appliqué cross and golden-threaded INRI embroidered on the back. Fully robed, Father Walt is wondrous to behold. When he was named chief priest at the cathedral, out went the old vestments, in came new ones, the most splendid ones in the history of my home town. They're silk, satin, brocade, velvet, colour-coded to the seasons and feasts and special celebrations of the liturgical year. Father Walt places a stiff, black three-cornered hat called a biretta on his head, puts one hand around the stem of his chalice beneath its draperies, places the other hand on top, turns, nods at me. I take my place in front of him and lead our small procession to the rear of the altar. I yank hard on the purple velvet bell rope. Father Walt likes a loud warning sounded. The organist switches from a bit of Bach to a hymn tune. We step into the sanctuary. Bodies clatter in the pews as they rise, and their voices throw gravel against the melody. A row of nuns at the front find their feet and the tune as smoothly as if all their working parts were lubricated daily with 3-in-One oil. I don't sing. I use the processional as a breathing space, a time in which I can remind myself of all the actions I must do. Today, I'm doing double duty; the second altar boy overslept. We genuflect in front of the altar. There is a sharp pain in my knee but I don't wince; Latin is already on my tongue as I kneel on the first step of the altar.

Introibo ad altare Dei, Father Walt says. I will go to the altar of God.

Ad Deum qui laetificat iuventutem meum, I respond. To God, who gives joy to my youth.

And there was much joy in my youth. I was not a happy child, not in the conventional sense. I was often frightened, frequently lonely, an odd little worrier, acutely shy, self-conscious. But I had a wonderful, amazing capacity for joy. I still have it, a wild, peculiar joy that erupts unexpectedly, sometimes at odd moments.

"There's nothing wrong with your knee," Roman says. Roman is my doctor. He's also my friend. "The chronic pain in it is displaced. From your back. There's some deterioration in your lower back, and the pain is registering in your left knee. I've got the same problem myself." He recommends that I wrap my knee in an elasticized bandage. This should reduce the pressure enough to break the neural connection. When I try it, it works reasonably well. But that's later. "Were you ever told," Roman continues, "that your spine never fully closed over?"

"No." I start to worry immediately.

"You've lived with it a long time. You don't need to start worrying about it now. Here, I'll show you what it looks like," he says, taking out the X-rays of my knee and back that the radiography lab had taken the previous week. "They weren't good at detecting spina bifida when we were children. Your family doctor missed it. It's fairly minor in your case. You do know what it is, don't you?"

I nod, but uncertainly. I know it puts children in wheelchairs from which they have a hard time ever escaping. I also know that the great country singer Hank Williams, who died in the fifties, had undiagnosed *spina bifida occulta,* became addicted to painkillers, and was ruined by them.

"Spina bifida is a congenital defect in the vertebrae. When the arch in a vertebra fails to develop, the spinal cord is unprotected and may be damaged. You're just lucky you didn't get hit hard playing sports when your back is most vulnerable. You could have been paralyzed. But you don't like contact sports, do you?"

I feel the blood drain from my face, my legs go weak; an odd sensation in my digestive system tells me I'm going to throw up. I also feel as if I'm going to faint. And then the nausea passes and I begin to smile. I'm grinning.

Roman is used to patients looking happy. He's a remarkable healer. But he doesn't know that he's just healed a very old wound. I'm feeling very, very good — so good that I have difficulty explaining myself.

"It's too complicated," I say finally. "I'm going to have to write it out."

"And put it in a book?"

"I'll put it in a book."

"And mention me?"

"I'll put you in it."

Roman is a big fan of my writing, and I am a big fan of his doctoring. We'd be closer friends if we had more in common. Like sports. Roman is an avid tennis player in the summer, a skier in the winter. A gifted high-school athlete, he had put most of his energy into boxing, his way of dealing with the anger and frustrations of an adolescence complicated by being a Jewish immigrant from Russia at the height of the Cold War. Even so, I envy him his training and experience in the ring. If I'd played sports, I'd have boxed, like my late cousin Rocky Wagner, who was a contender for middleweight champion of the Allied armies in Europe. But I don't play any sports. I keep in shape riding stationary bicycles, lifting weights, and working with medicine balls at my local Y. And I've only been doing that for a dozen years. Mostly, I walk. I've always walked. Shank's pony, my father called it.

When I was a child, I walked at a trot. Sometimes I galloped, but I rarely ran. I ran awkwardly, gingerly, slowly, because when I ran, my left knee hurt. Children in those days were allowed to hurt ourselves falling down or off things, and then we were allowed to feel bruised, but we weren't expected to have stabbing pains in our knees or elsewhere when we were otherwise healthy.

Our family doctor said, "He's making it up. He'll run better when his left foot straightens enough for him to wear running shoes. Until then, put him in Sisman Scampers. All he needs now is a specially shaped heel. One like this." And he drew an odd shape on his prescription pad and wrote something and handed the sheet to my mother. "Mr. Fritz knows exactly how to shape them. Make your boy play outdoors. He'll run. He'll straighten out."

I ran only when I was being chased. By bullies. By dogs. By unnameable fears. I couldn't run the bases with any skill. That hardly mattered, since I could hardly ever hit the ball. My father the baseball fan said, "You don't have to worry about that. You're a natural leftie. We'll make a pitcher out of you." And he tried to turn me into the lefthander of his dreams on lazy Sunday afternoons in the alley behind our house. I threw, my big brother caught, and my father coached a kid who just couldn't get the motions right. On good Sundays, my eldest sister's boyfriend Jim, who could really pitch and pitched a lot of small town tournament games, showed me how to do it. In the excitement of watching Jim deliver his sizzling fastball with pinpoint accuracy to my brother's under-padded catcher's mitt, my father would forget about me, and I'd slip away and read a book, maybe *Treasure Island,* maybe *Robinson Crusoe.*

THREE

An Island of Treasures

I'm not one of the Tara Lipinskys of this world. Unlike the 1998 Olympic Gold Medalist in Women's Figure Skating, I didn't climb up on a makeshift podium when I was two years old and announce a grand plan for my life and then go out and make it happen. If I had, you wouldn't be reading this, and I'd be a plumber billing somebody sixty-five bucks an hour for unblocking a drain or installing a new kitchen sink. At two, I wasn't telling anybody anything: I was keeping my dreams of pipe threaders and blowtorches to myself. At three, same thing. Family legend has it that I only began to speak more than the odd word when I was four. My first word isn't remembered by anyone, not reliably. I'd say it was probably "truck." When I was four, I really wanted to go places with a big tool box, and I couldn't imagine a better way of travelling than in a dark green half-ton. A Ford. Then I learned to read. F-o-r-d, except the F seemed to me to look the wrong way round unless it was written in the flowing cursive script of the Ford logo.

I was reading after a fashion — the words I could not decode, I just omitted — before I started school, coached by a tag team of my five older sisters, who helped me to do what they had been taught to do in the classrooms of Holy Rosary school: sound out words. My big brother — who took me places where he wanted to go and I was glad to follow — was too impatient for this. He loved numbers more than words; he and I counted things. My first book was Helen Bannerman's *The Story of Little Black Sambo*. It's racist, right? Not for me, not then. "Sambo" sounded a whole lot better to my ear than the pet name the adult world put upon me — "Butch" — and I loved the idea of skin as dark as Fry's chocolate. But most of all, I loved that boy's energy, his sense of adventure, courage, and cunning. When Sambo tricked the tigers into chasing each other so fast around a tree that they turned to butter, I was hooked on books that told stories. A dark green half-ton, fine as it was, couldn't turn a tiger into butter, a small boy into a great hero. S-a-m-b-o t-i-g-e-r b-u-t-t-e-r. Then Joel Chandler Harris's *Uncle Remus. Brer Rabbit. Brer Fox.* The words I could not see clearly because they did not stay still on the page, I just ignored.

My big brother was and is four years older, a hero to me then and now. On a cold winter's day filled with falling snow (a day I can still taste on the tip of my tongue whenever an oversize snowflake lands there), sometime between Christmas 1949 and Epiphany 1950 — I was five and he, with an early January birthday, may well have just turned ten — my big brother took me to a library for the first time in my life. He pulled me on a toboggan, and I held on to an empty cardboard box and a piece of blanket so they would not fall off. Setting out from home at number 209, we travelled up the hill of Angus Crescent and along College Avenue to Elphinstone Street, where we stopped to have a snowball fight and an adventure in and among the freight cars and sheds of the Monarch Lumber Company. My big brother pulled me up Elphinstone all the way to Thirteenth Avenue and the Connaught Branch of the Regina Public Library.

It was the first time I'd ever been inside a public building that wasn't Holy Rosary Cathedral or a shop. I was overawed.

I don't remember precisely the books we sledded home in that box covered with that blanket on that toboggan, but I walked and pulled and my brother talked to a friend he'd met there. I was too happy for words. At home, I do remember this exchange between my mother and brother: "He's not old enough for these. There are too many words. Why didn't you help him find some picture books?"

"I tried to, but he didn't want them. He wanted these. You know how he is!"

Oh, how I was, indeed! Stubbornly, I wrestled with the books the library allowed me to take home on my brother's card, since I wasn't eligible for a card of my own until I started school. Those books, whichever they were, had black-and-white illustrations of ships and sailors and villainous pirates at the head of each chapter and full-page colour illustrations at regular intervals and many, many words that I could not read, but those unknown words made them exactly what I've ever after wanted books to be — beyond my depth, unfathomable at first reading, as rich with diverse lives, half-seen and half-hidden, as the Grand Banks off Newfoundland were then said to be. Books from which I netted new experiences and ever more enriching experiences the more I trawled them. Books bursting with images and imagery, books overflowing with old words *just out* to those who have not heard them.

Hispaniola.

Hispaniola — the good ship upon which Master Jim Hawkins sets forth from the Admiral Benbow Inn with Cap'n Flint and the others in search of Treasure Island. Robert Louis Stevenson's *Treasure Island* was mine at eight, the first real book I remember owning. It was a secondhander from my brother, who thought he had outgrown it. I did not think I'd outgrown it until I was eighteen and at university in Saskatoon, a first year student in arts, majoring in philosophy. I was mistaken then: I still have not outgrown it.

My last year of high school, 1961-1962. Oh, what a school year that was! Not the year I'd expected, not at all. I was ill, too sick in body and in heart for school much of the time. Six weeks of hospital care — three weeks in November, another three in January. A severe kidney infection in the days when powerful antibiotics could only be administered by needle. Two in each buttock, three times a day until my backside was bruised black, blue, purple, and yellow.

"My verbosity is superdeligorgeous, to be hypospondulically explicit," said the old man in the hospital bed next to mine. Every morning. First words and second and third of the day, day after day, three weeks full. He was a madman, a horror, and I fled from him into other words.

"It's crackers to slip a rozzer the dropsky in snide," said I in my favourite reply, quoting the marginalia of *Mad* magazine. I was as puffed up with motley words as a bumful of penicillin:

> Buck Mulligan came from the stairhead, bearing a bowl of lather on which a mirror and a razor lay crossed. A yellow dressing gown, ungirdled, was sustained gently behind him by the mild morning air. He held the bowl aloft and intoned: *Introibo ad altare Dei.*

James Joyce. Catholic words. A Catholic world. Thomas Merton. G.K. Chesterton. A Buddhist world, too (if Allan Watts can be called Buddhist). Zen and Beat — oh, so beatnik — Jack Kerouac. Ginsberg. *Howl.* My hospital bed, my bedroom at home — nests of books! And to escape the howls of the verbose monster in the next bed and the monstrous dropskys inside my own, *Hispaniola,* a good ship upon which Master Jim Hawkins and I — a better I than the eye in my bed saw in the mirror, aye — set forth from the Admiral Benbow Inn with Cap'n Flint and the others in search of Treasure Island. I read Robert Louis Stevenson's *Treasure Island* and *Kidnapped,* Kipling's *Kim,* Twain's *Tom Sawyer, Huckleberry Finn, The Prince and Pauper,* and *Puddin'head Wilson,* Dumas's *The Three Musketeers,* and Dickens's *Oliver Twist* and *A Tale of Two Cities* again that final year of high school, a last grasp at the past that had been mine as a schoolboy who hated school and sports and loved books.

The Connaught Branch of the Regina Public Library and its librarians — all misses to me regardless of their marital status — loom large and lovely: Miss Fullerton, who gave me my first card; Miss Young, who tried to keep me from growing older too quickly; Miss McKinnon, who nourished my appetite for books like another woman might educate a child to the tastes of adult cuisine. And Miss Hanssen, who was employed there only long enough for a small boy to fall hopelessly into infatuation with a full-grown woman for the first time. Under their eyes at the Connaught, I read the shelves according to a plan. I'd seek out stories (whose bare outlines I already knew, had visualized from Illustrated Classics comic books) that were exactly what I've ever after wanted tales to be — adventures in reading beyond my depth: *The Man in the Iron Mask, The Hunchback of Notre Dame, Don Quixote, Men Against the Sea, Swiss Family Robinson, Robinson Crusoe*. I now know that *Robinson Crusoe* is much more than a story filled with risky enterprises and daring feats, but that's how I first read this "true story" of a shipwrecked sailor marooned on a tropical island. But even reading it realistically, ignoring Daniel Defoe's authorship completely, thinking of it as Crusoe speaking directly to me as the narrator of "The Life and Strange Surprizing Adventures of Robinson Crusoe of York, Mariner ... Written by Himself," I understood that this book was giving voice to a theme with large implications for my own life, the competition between the human need for society and the equally powerful yearning for solitude. What I didn't get from it at all (possibly because I may have read it in an expurgated and abridged version designed for children or, more likely, because personal conversion, "being saved," played little part in the Catholic view of salvation) is that it is also a tale of religious transformation filled with veiled references to Dissenters such as Defoe himself. Crusoe asserts that Christianity can be rebuilt with little more than a repentant heart, and that his struggles on a tropical island represent a soul's journey through the wilderness of a fallen world to a place of deliverance by means of repentance and conversion. But I may also have missed this point for another reason: *Robinson Crusoe* is a work that enlightens as it startles. It does precisely what Coleridge says of it: "Now this is De Foe's excellence. You become a man while you read." Defoe is broader, more universal in his humanity than in his Christianity. Reading for me was a way of finding my way into being a kind of man other than my father was: a man needy for society and little given to solitude.

My father does not strike me in retrospect as a man who enjoyed novels unless they were explicitly religious in nature. I do remember him reading Jim Bishop's *The Day Christ Died* with considerable pleasure. Bishop, a veteran newsman, retells the gospel story as reportage and interviews. My father liked newspapers and news broadcasts, loved facts and the analysis of facts. He did not like to see me losing myself in books and imagining things. He did not want to know that I thought of our neighbourhood as an island, bordered by Elphinstone Street on the west, 13th Avenue to the north, the west side of Albert Street to the east, and Wascana Creek to the south, and myself as a Crusoe within it. But that was what it was to me. Everything within those hundred or so city blocks — Connaught Library, Holy Rosary Cathedral, Holy Rosary School, Sacred Heart Academy, various small shops, and the homes of my friends — was mine to explore and discover, to scavenge for odd bits of lumber and metal I could put to some fantastic purpose. Until I was eleven and had learned to ride the red and white Schwinn bicycle I'd inherited from my big brother, I did not journey beyond the limits of that island on my own. To travel across the wild seas of the rest of the city or to venture onto the flood plain, the hayfields, and the links of the Gyro Citizens' Golf Club south of the creek and west of Elphinstone always required companions — sometimes my big brother, sometimes my pal Billy with his dog Rusty.

My father liked it even less when I shrank that island of mine to the single curve of our street and thought Angus Crescent a wagon train of Métis on a buffalo hunt. I galloped then, and my father did not like me galloping through his house or past his neighbours, wearing a cowboy hat, packing six-shooters, imagining things.

FOUR

A New Year in Saskatchewan

Picture this: a boy, me, ten years, eight months, seven days old, warming himself by sitting sideways on the cast iron radiator beneath the double window at the north end of the living room of our house at 209 Angus Crescent, Regina, Saskatchewan, Dominion of Canada, British Commonwealth of Nations, North America, Planet Earth, the Solar System, the Milky Way. It is January 1, 1955, and this boy, me, is just in from outside, just home from the cathedral, where he, an altar boy, has assisted at an evening service of Benediction. Saskatchewan and all its people have been blessed by Archbishop O'Neill on the first day of its fiftieth anniversary. I know, I do know the official date of the province's birth is September 1, but some people can't wait to count their blessings.

This boy, me, is blessed with a capacity to daydream, and although he is sitting there on the radiator, surrounded by a large, active family which is readying itself to have its photograph taken in an informal family portrait, he is still outside, and snow is falling. The wind is rising, and a blizzard is coming, and the radiator is an Indian pony, a pinto, and he, no longer me, is Paul not Terry, Savard not Rigelhof, the son of a buffalo hunter not a provincial civil servant, Metis not *Volgadeutsch*. And Paul Savard doesn't know where he is or if he will ever find his way home. Paul had known where he was when he was with his family in North Dakota, but he became separated from them in the heat of a buffalo hunt when they crossed over into Montana, and he alone was captured by a band of Assiniboine and taken north. And Paul has escaped on this pony, and he's in Canada and not very many miles from where Terry sits on the radiator, but there is nothing and no one to tell him that he is in another country and that the country he is in will become Saskatchewan when there are no more buffalo to hunt. Paul is lost, but he has unknowingly found his way to the place to which the buffalo bones will be hauled as a cash crop and piled so high that they become the dominant marker in the landscape until they are shipped to the button and fertilizer factories of Chicago: Wascana, "Pile-o'-Bones," the grandiose Regina, its capital.

Saskatchewan is as artificial, as made up, as Paul Savard, with political boundaries unrelated to geographical regions. Neither rivers nor lakes nor ranges of hills nor peculiar rock nor soils distinguish the boundaries between Saskatchewan and adjacent provinces and states:

> Parallel of latitude 60 is Saskatchewan's northern boundary. This mathematical line of measurement runs through lake, rock, muskeg, bush country, and sub-Arctic tundra . . . similar to the terrain of the contiguous Northwest Territories. Along Saskatchewan's southern border, the 49th parallel, North Dakota's grain land and Montana's grazing country merge so naturally with those of Saskatchewan, a roving horseman might not know whether he was in the Canadian province or either of the American states, unless reminded by a customs or immigration patrol.
>
> From Saskatchewan's southern to northern boundary is 761 miles. The southern east-west boundary is 393 miles in length, the northern 277.

We do not measure distances in miles any longer — it is 1225 kilometres from Saskatchewan's southern to northern boundary and the southern east-west boundary is 665 kilometres in length, the northern 446. I also know that the land north of 60 is Nunavut now, but I'm reading from *Saskatchewan: The History of a Province,* by J.F.C. Wright, published by McClelland and Stewart in 1955 to commemorate the Golden Jubilee of the Province of Saskatchewan. The habit of making others' words part of my own came to me early. Paul Savard was my alter ego all those years ago, but not my invention — he is the hero of my favourite book of 1955, that year of Jubilee, Mary Weekes's novel *Painted Arrows.*

Saskatchewan is artificial, but people made of it something real and special, a place that was being written into existence with a past and a present and a future and taught to its children in its schools and re-imagined over and over and over again in the years of my childhood.

> Opportunity-seeking, land-eager, restless, underprivileged, and idealistic people came to the Canadian prairies from many lands and for a variety of reasons. . . . [T]hose who stayed were unavoidably conditioned by the intractable geography, uncertain economy, and emergent social consciousness of a frontier sparsely populated by men and women who brought with them various and numerous predilections and customs, while all in common were faced with the need to learn rapidly new ways for survival and success in a new and untried land.

That too is Wright.

Paul dismounted from that pony double-quick and hit the carpet as Terry eagerly flew to the back porch and returned silently with a screwdriver and pliers the moment the tripod holding the camera began to sway and my brother's arm shot out from under his photographer's black hood and struggled to steady a wobbly wooden leg. My brother, then almost fifteen, a first-year high-school student and a member of the Photography Club at Campion College, had borrowed a large-format camera with all its attachments: the heavy wood and brass tripod, the black hood, twin floodlights, photographic plates, and a mechanical remote shutter control. That allowed him to place himself within the frame of an image that would squeeze our family down to four inches by five inches, reduce it to black and white, and freeze it at one moment of its existence so that it could be enlarged and printed double size in the college's darkroom and given back to us to become a page in one of my mother's many photograph albums.

The child is father of the man. We all knew then that my brother would always be a manipulator of mechanical devices and a maker of things. But what precisely he would make of himself and his place in the world around him in the next half century was not clear to any of us in that room. If there had been a seer among us and she had said that forty-seven years later, in 2002, he would celebrate his thirty-fifth anniversary as a member of McGill University's Department of Mathematics, I would not have been surprised. He was forever attempting to explain to me how things worked, from kitchen faucets to football plays, with diagrams and formulae. But had such a prophetess been so specific as to say that my brother would lead graduate seminars in such things as the study of fractyls, write computer programs, and spend several years overseeing the implementation of a multi-million-dollar software program for the integration of his university's networks and systems, most of her words would have been gibberish and the tens of millions of dollars in his budget much too marvellous to believe.

The child is father of the man. There are people in the photograph taken in that room that night (and there was no fortune teller among my parents and siblings) who will say that it is no surprise to any of them that the younger of the two boys in the picture, me, the out-of-breath one who had not paused to comb his hair, would become a teacher and a writer. But the kinds of things I teach and the books I write and the fact that I choose to do both in Montreal does continue to surprise most of them. As a child, I seemed to myself and to them altogether too rooted in Angus Crescent and Regina and Saskatchewan to ever move very far away, too religious to ever become quite so god-less, and far too serious to become so quirkily humorous. I was a child of that neighbourhood, and it was a healthy and safe place to live. It interested me vitally.

Only one of my father and mother's eight children — the eldest — has lived and continues to live her adult life in Regina, and her house is miles to the north and west of our childhood home. The area of Saskatchewan is greater than the combined area of England and Germany, but it was too small to contain seven of the eight children who grew up in that house on Angus Crescent. We moved away and settled — one in Victoria, one in Surrey, one in Edmonton, two in Calgary, two in Montreal — like ever so many thousands of the Joni Mitchell generation, our generation, a generation which has looked at life from both sides, never knowing where we stood, going round and round, looking for a big yellow taxi with the right sort of radio to take us far beyond Woodstock and other people's parties as we courted and sparked in shadows and light to the hissing of summer lawns in a dog-eat-dog world, building lives that might have more substance than a chalk mark in a rainstorm. My brother tells me that he's been in touch via the Internet with some of his fellow graduates in engineering physics from the University of Saskatchewan's Faculty of Engineering, class of 1962. He tells me that most of his classmates have travelled much further from Saskatoon than Montreal and are people with international reputations in oceanography, nuclear energy, and several other technical fields. And he laughs as he remembers that he once had to explain the intricacies of the Saskatoon public transit system to some of them — a bunch of boys fresh from the farm, and he the only big city kid among them.

Picture this: that small boy, me, ten years, eight months, seven days old, that same night, but now keeping himself warm by wrapping himself in a patchwork quilt, sitting on a wooden chair at the gable window in the highest part of the house on Angus Crescent. That house has a full attic, unheated and unfinished, cold, dusty, and magical. It was a place where my brother and I often went to play and to which this boy, me, sneaks away in the middle of the night. I have a telescope, a small, folding telescope with a magnification power of three, more than enough to see ever so much of the starry night. After midnight all the buses have stopped running, all the street lights are extinguished, and this child only ever sees the occasional sickroom window illuminated anywhere in his neighbourhood. He wants to be alone with the stars, and he is. He does not even seek out the constellations his brother has taught him to find. He wants to be alone with the stars in their millions of millions. He has been taught that there is a star for every person who has ever lived on Angus Crescent, in Regina, in Saskatchewan, in the Dominion of Canada, in the Commonwealth, in North America, on Planet Earth of the Solar System in the Milky Way, and more stars for all of those who have yet to be born. He has been taught that the stars are very old and that, in looking at them, he is seeing very far back into the past, into all our beginnings. Long before Joni Mitchell ever sang it, he knew that we are truly, literally stardust.

The stretch of time backwards extends so far beyond normal comprehension that to grasp some sense of it, that boy was taught, as a Jubilee gift from Professor Wright, to consider the two billion year history of planet earth as one year only, beginning, as calendar years always do, on January 1. In that hypothetical year, it took until the end of March for the earth's surface to cool enough to form great oceans, including the immense and shallow sea that covered Saskatchewan and deposited potassium salts which remained when the waters eventually evaporated. At the end of June (a billion years ago), mineral-eating micro-organisms living without benefit of direct sunlight appeared in warm ocean basins. In mid-November (more than nine thousand million years ago), fernlike trees were growing in the great marshes. When the trees died and fell in the waters, they joined the remains of huge reptiles, silted over, and formed coal beds and oil fields. By mid-December (70 million years ago), giant dinosaurs walked erect. Two days before Christmas, the Rocky Mountains buckled upwards from the collision of the earth's tectonic plates. On December 31, on other continents, the first human beings emerged.

> In the late evening of the same day, about 9:40 p.m. (600,000 years ago) came the first great glacier grinding down from the north. At approximately 10:25 o'clock began a second glacial period, followed by a third at 11:15 p.m., and then a fourth and possibly a fifth. . . . Close to midnight of that last day of this hypothetical year (20,000 to 30,000 years ago), across the Bering Straits from Asia came those nomadic hunters, the prehistoric Indians. Some three seconds before midnight, the first European explorers and fur traders were paddling up the Saskatchewan River. And a fraction of a second before midnight, as if awaiting the cheers to usher in New Year's Day, Saskatchewan became a province of Canada.

And at a fraction of a second after midnight, when Saskatchewan is about to become one hundred years old, within a fraction of that fraction, a man who is still a boy recalls a fraction of a fraction in its landscape, the house at 209 Angus Crescent, Regina, Saskatchewan, Dominion of Canada, the Commonwealth, North America, Planet Earth, the Solar System, the Milky Way. Our old home is now the Mitchell house. The writer Ken Mitchell bought it and built an insulated study in its attic, where he has imagined his plays and stories and brought them into being.

In April 1955, when the boy I was turned eleven, George W. Simpson was head of the history department at the University of Saskatchewan. He had begun his life ploughing with oxen on a homestead south of Swift Current before becoming a teacher in a one-room schoolhouse near Ponteix, his first step up the professional ladder that led to Saskatoon. In his introduction to Wright's *Saskatchewan: The History of a Province,* he wrote:

> In one sense the history of Saskatchewan reflects distantly the pulsations of European history in one of its most vital periods of growth. When Europe wanted furs, a tremor of activity ran along Saskatchewan's rivers, through her forests, and over her great plains. . . . As Europe and Eastern America became industrialized, her plains were used for cattle or ploughed up for wheat and other grains; prospectors searched the north for essential metals; and vast new systems of transportation were established to meet the new developing forms of economic life.
>
> European reflection was to be seen not only in economic affairs . . . and . . . the framework of our political life. The religious movements and organizations of Europe were carried here by devoted men, while other cultural institutions, vogues, fashions, and trends ultimately reached this western periphery.
>
> Saskatchewan's history, however, cannot be regarded simply as a distant reflection of movements originating elsewhere. It has its own unique quality and pattern.

There are far too many capitalized nouns in the vocabulary of Wright's book — especially words like "Whiteman" and "Halfbreed" and "Indian." It is a book of its time, and its time was tribalist and racialist. The boy in the photograph, the younger of the two boys in the picture, me, the out-of-breath one who had not paused to comb his hair, the one who would become a teacher and a writer, resisted those tribal markers, hated all that racialist naming and name-calling. He hated collective nouns passionately and turned away from as many group activities as he possibly could unless bullied into joining. He loved the specific, the individuated, the idiosyncratic, the exceptional, the distinguishing details. He loved looking through the windows of the house on Angus Crescent. At night, in its attic, he thought he could see forever.

The photograph I have just described does not in fact exist outside these pages. While I was writing it into being, I thought something very like it did exist. I thought the only liberty I was taking was in having my brother trigger the camera's shutter on January 1, 1955, for dramatic effect. I believed it had been taken a couple of days earlier. And then I looked in my mother's photo albums and found that I have made one photograph out of two separate images and that, so far as the photographer or anyone else remembers, neither was taken in 1955. A photograph in which my hair is uncombed and I have just returned from altar boy duties at Sunday evening Benediction and glow with happiness was taken before my brother knew how to use the remote device. He's not in it, nor are some of my sisters. The other photograph, with him in it and me catching my breath, is an almost full family portrait — only Sister Mary Helen, my second-eldest sister, who departed for the convent when she was seventeen, is missing. By the time it was taken, I had become my father's son in at least a couple of ways, and I don't look quite so happy. But I did not make up the bit about watching the stars from the attic window on January 1, 1955. I did do that. I did a lot of star-gazing throughout 1955, and I saved my money to buy a good telescope until I got interested in the red-hot syncopations of Jelly Roll

Morton, Louis Armstrong and Fats Waller, Woody Guthrie's dust bowl songs, and Leadbelly's blues and Fats Domino's New Orleans stride piano, and I bought a record player instead.

FIVE

Glory Days

Somewhere in this world there must be another such as I, a man with five older sisters, an older brother, a younger sister. I've never met nor heard of him. Birth order is said to explain a lot; I don't doubt it. In my five years in seminaries in Saskatoon and Ottawa, I met many whose personalities were not unlike my own, especially among francophones from Northern Ontario, New England, Quebec. Like me, most came from large — sometimes extremely large — families. Again, like me, some nursed a sense of being slightly defective and physically awkward. I found myself among others who stumbled when we moved quickly, stammered and said things the wrong way round when we spoke under pressure. What we did best was to sit still and say little until we had command of ourselves and the situation. As children, we'd all loved to sit by a window and watch the interplay of sun and clouds or winds and rain on the sidewalks and roadways and passersby outside our houses. Or watch the stars in the night sky.

There was one place where our stillness and quiet, our slow, precise ways of speaking, our unhurried movements were more than welcome, and that was at church. We became very good at the rituals of our religion. Being altar boys brought enormous pleasure and pride, success and status. Serving the priests in the performance of the sacramental rites with proper deportment, decorum, ceremony, clarity, and precision earned praise and parental pride. It also rained gifts on us. There were prayer cards and holy medals from newly ordained priests, expensive rosaries from Rome and the Holy Land (including one with what was said to be an authentic sliver of the true cross inside the crucifix), breaks from school routine when we were called out of class for funerals, and lavish breakfasts at rectories and convents where housekeepers or nuns prepared bacon and eggs however we wanted them and added sausages and ham and pancakes as well. And pocket money. Serving at weddings and funerals brought sealed envelopes with crisp new bills inside. For me, there was even a small cigar once from a papal delegate from Rome, who insisted that I smoke it and sip cognac with him at a convent in the middle of a school day when my classmates were doing algebra. But that was later, in my adolescence. The Monsignor from the Vatican wanted to loosen my tongue and get answers to his questions about a priest who was of particular interest to Papal authorities; what I said was secret, and he thanked me with a twenty-dollar bill — roughly equivalent to $150 today. I remember using it to buy a pair of Levi's boot-cut jeans, a crewneck sweater, and a Miles Davis LP, *Kind of Blue.*

Some of my primary school friends teased me about all the time I spent in church. They thought I was trying to show them up by being too good. I didn't see it that way at all. I was well-behaved but angry inside. Dyslexia is more than a reading disorder; the reading disorder is only a symptom of a deeper condition. If the reading disorder is overcome, dyslexia doesn't disappear. It never goes away because it's fundamentally an aberrant gene, a technical failure to keep proper timing in the circuits of the body's audio-visual system. The visual system has two components — one for fast processes like motion, depth perception, three-dimensional vision, the other for slow processes like colour, stationary images, detail. Dyslexics respond much better to the latter. It can be the same with sound — dyslexics are good on long tones, poor on short, likelier to prefer Miles Davis's solos to John Coltrane's. For dyslexics, when things are slowed down, our responses are the same as everyone else's. But usually life doesn't move at our speed, and we rarely see and hear exactly what is going on around us. There's always some difficulty in picking up conversational cues and visual signals. We rarely feel absolutely certain, totally confident. If we miss too much, are confronted with unexpected questions too frequently, we become passive and wait for things to happen and get angry with an anger that turns in on itself, burning straight down to the deepest reaches of our feelings about ourselves. Especially when there's no alternative to acting swiftly. Every athletic endeavour is a potential nightmare.

On Saturday afternoons, my family joined the lines outside Holy Rosary Cathedral's four confessionals. I was never in a hurry, liked to confess after my father and my sisters had their say. They, already cleansed, prayed their penances in the pews or on the steps at the side altars in the light of flickering blue votive candles while I pulled the padded leather door shut behind me, creating total darkness, and felt my way forward and down to the kneeler, pressed my nose against the mesh screen, heard muffled voices saying serious things very softly. One little wooden window slid shut, and the other one, the one on my side scraped open. Cough-drop breath, talcum powder, tired eyes, quivering ear hairs, a priest who is not Father Walt and fastidious, some more lenient confessor from the Franciscan priory.

"Bless me Father for I have sinned. It has been a week since my last confession. Since that time I have . . ." and I recite my sins in a list.

There is anger, anger, always more anger to be confessed, and the lies, lies, lies I've told to mask it. In two, three minutes it's done. The friar offers kind words of advice I'll try to follow but won't find very helpful, and I say my act of contrition as he gives absolution in Latin, our voices simultaneous and dissonant. He, whoever it is, always finishes first. "Go in peace," he says, and before I'm gone, someone else is blurting out other less angry things on the other side of the box.

I'm not at peace with myself except when I am reading a book or serving at the altar. In a very good week, I might make it through to the end of Sunday breakfast without an inner explosion of rage, fury at myself. I had no idea then, nor for a long time afterwards, that I'd been born with an aberrant gene on chromosome six. When you know what to expect, dyslexia is less of a problem.

Father Walt did not like the unexpected to occur on the altar during services at the cathedral. Altar boys assembled twice a week for general rehearsals, were called out of school to rehearse for Easter week celebrations. He singled out some of us for special attention and drilled us in posture and movement, and oh how wonderfully I progressed under his training. And oh how he rewarded me by asking me to serve at funerals that took me out of class on schoolday mornings and Saturday weddings that put money in my pockets.

My career at the altar began at an unusually young age. As a five-year-old, I was selected to carry a statue of the infant Jesus, a doll really, on a purple pillow with gold braid and tassels in the archbishop's procession to the elaborate manger surrounded by Christmas trees at St. Joseph's side altar, a ritual that marked the start of Midnight Mass on Christmas Eve through all the years I attended services at Holy Rosary Cathedral. I had yet to make my First Communion, but I was thought too innocent to have ever sinned. I was also just the right size for the purple cassock and the starched white lace blouse in the cathedral's clothes closet. I was still the right size a year later, when I was officially a member of the altar boy society. By the time I'd made my First Communion at Easter of first grade at Holy Rosary School, I'd memorized the Latin responses well enough to serve alongside older boys at morning Mass:

> *Introibo ad altare Dei.*
> *Ad Deum qui laetificat iuventutem meum.*

By grade two, I was big enough to wear the larger purple cassock and lace blouse set aside for the boy who carried the train of the archbishop's ermine-trimmed purple velvet cape and kept it out of the way of his gold-embroidered white silk shoes, a worrisome task.

Because it was the cathedral parish, the services at Holy Rosary were unusually elaborate and made more baroque and princely by an appetite for the regal and ceremonial shared by the archbishop and Father Walt. There were three Masses daily and five on Sunday, including an Episcopal High Mass at ten o'clock with a full Procession and Throne. An altar boy could aspire to rise through the ranks of Episcopal High Mass participants, from merely marching in the procession to taking such active roles as one of six white-gowned and red-caped torch bearers, or one of a pair of acolytes, the candle bearers. He might earn promotion and carry the episcopal cross upright at the head of the procession, or dangle the thurible (the incense burner) at his side, or hold the censer (the pot containing the incense), or the mitre (the white and gold high-peaked hat the archbishop put on over his purple skullcap at several points in the Mass), or the crosier (the symbolic gold-plated shepherd's crook), or the oversized episcopal liturgical book. Top rank, the highest you could go as an altar boy, was to be appointed master of ceremonies and cue all the others. In time, I played all the roles. And because I was good at them, faithful and punctual, I was asked to serve at the archbishop's private chapel in his home on weekdays and to breakfast with him. While I remained prepubescent, pretty and soprano-voiced, I served at a lot of Saturday morning weddings — more than a hundred. It was a lot of work, but it was God's work, and my father was more tolerant of my book-reading and daydreaminess because of it.

Whenever I rewind my memories and turn back half a century to the mid-fifties, when I was nine and ten and a devout and devoted altar boy, or even to 1962, when I entered the seminary at eighteen, an odd thing happens. It all replays as a silent movie, one in which I can mime all the actions. I enter churches as rarely as I can (funerals can't be avoided and become depressingly common in everyone's sixth decade), and whenever I do, my hands remember how to sign the cross and my knees to genuflect. Five minutes ago, I stood up from my desk and let my arms do the motions necessary for handling a cross, candle, crosier, mitre, thurible, censer, and book, and the smaller, defter gestures of the master of ceremonies. It's all there in my body, available at instant recall. In front of an altar, I can still choreograph the whole of a High Mass mentally, play the roles of the priest and the altar boys, make all the movements. But after the priest says, "I will go to the altar of God," and the congregation replies, "To God who brings joy to my youth," there's silence. The sentences of the Mass, Latin and English, that I could say entirely from memory, beginning to end, the prayers, the hymns, almost everything that I learned by rote to accompany ritual actions is gone, erased. The Greek *Kyrie eleison* and fragments of the *Agnus Dei* and *Gloria* remain in Latin, but this has more to do with listening to recordings of Bach Masses than with the memory of church services. The prayers I do remember — the Lord's Prayer and the Magnificat — are taken from the New Testament, which I still read. Otherwise, it's as if, when I abandoned the rituals, my mind utterly rebelled against the routine recitation of the language of ritual. The silence isn't inexpressive. Sometimes, standing in a church, I do feel the old feelings. I feel safe and protected. I even feel oddly loved.

Oddly loved?

The families who worshipped at Holy Rosary Cathedral and sent their sons and daughters to Holy Rosary School (the buildings stand back-to-back on the same city block, with the rectory and its garages between them) carried names like Achen, Moynihan, Leibel, McCarthy,

McNeill, MacDonald, Curran, Ryan, Leveille, Beaudry, Pyck, Mayer, Brennan, Petrie, Toupin, Blender, Burns, Strachan, Moriarty, Gottselig, Tourigny, Chapdelaine, Goulet, Riffel, Warnke, Gates, Toth, Shaw, Hill, Cels, Scott, Collins, Roberts, Robertson, Tracy, Hengen, Schmidt, Letourneau, Hanley, Morton, Yunker, Brhelle, Gosselin, Lalonde, Bolen, Kurtz, Dufour, Olsen, White, Charbonneau, Lecours, Coupal, Silinger, Fuchs, Castagner, Volk, Coyle, Lobsinger, Antonini, Braun, Alexander, Phelan, Dunne. We were a parish of Irish from Ireland, Montreal Irish, lowland Scots, Cape Breton Scots, French from Quebec, Métis from the Red River, Swiss, Italians, English from Manchester, Poles, Germans from Germany, and Germans from Russia. We were multicultural but didn't have the vocabulary then to think of ourselves as such. Many of us oscillated between homes where the language was French or German or Italian or Polish and school where only English was ever spoken and foreign-sounding phonemes were purged. But we were a people united by our religion: the One, True, Holy, Universal Roman Catholic Church. We were also outsiders, a minority that the Protestant majority resented and resisted and might turn against again, as they had after World War I, when the Ku Klux Klan came into Saskatchewan and made common cause with the Orange Lodges against Eastern Europeans, Catholics, and Jews. And because of that we were all Irish every St. Patrick's Day. And because of that we were a clan, and each of us had clan mothers and clan fathers who looked out for our welfare, sent us back home and phoned our parents when we looked as if we were up to no good or acted unruly. We were Catholics, and we were held to a higher standard. God was our Father and the church was our Mother, and every adult in the parish was to be obeyed as a parent, and parents were to do as the priests dictated. We were protected three times over, kept safe and loved. This was effective and even at times welcome when we were small and secretly glad to have our adventures reined in. We felt no personal vulnerability to religious antagonisms or to enmities as old as the Reformation and as all-encompassing as the Seven Year's War, the Clearances, the Famine, the Mackenzie-Papineau and Northwest rebellions.

We called priests "Father," and a priest like Father Walt understood himself to be the clan patriarch, a tribal chieftain. I must have heard him preach hundreds of Sunday sermons, but they have all merged into a homily on Mark 10:13-16:

> And they brought young children to him, that he should touch them: and his disciples rebuked those who brought them. But when Jesus saw it, he was much displeased, and said unto them, Suffer the little children to come unto me, and forbid them not: for of such is the kingdom of God. Verily I say unto you, Whosoever shall not receive the kingdom of God as a little child, he shall not enter therein. And he took them up in his arms, put his hands upon them, and blessed them.

This thought is so common in the gospels that a reader might think that Jesus meant what he said. Father Walt evidently thought so. What he had to say upon these words (and he could be eloquent in the saying of it) came back to this, always this: be pure in heart, mind, and body, do good deeds, give generously to your church, avoid places of sin, confess your sins, and receive Communion every Sunday. Before the start of Mass, he read announcements that enumerated the deeds to be done in the parish, the donations to be made to the church, the places of sin — the movies, the books, the teenage hangouts — to be avoided. At times in these announcements and always after Mass at the doors of the cathedral, Father Walt would single out for undivided attention those he thought immodest, ungenerous, or otherwise wandering from the straight and narrow. His words could be cruel and his manner mean, and he was probably as much loathed as loved, but Father Walt never allowed any priest working in his parish to physically or verbally abuse any altar boy without facing his wrath. Or to grow so friendly as to give a hug. If it happened once, it never happened a second time. Not on his watch. "Woe," he would say at the end of his sermon, "to those who give scandal. It would be better had they not been born."

SIX

The Making of a Paper Boy

Much more than the passage of time separates me now from the world of my youth. The lines of division move erratically in several directions, are smudged with erasures, but I can still pick out the jagged edges of the peaks and troughs of my adolescence. When I turned twelve, I began working as a paper boy delivering the afternoon edition of the Regina *Leader-Post*. My father was opposed to my doing this — Dad still hoped that I would wake up one day with a compulsion to play team sports like my brother, who joined baseball, football, and hockey teams in organized leagues. But my mother rightly insisted that this was never going to happen and that she didn't want me just hanging about the streets after school or moping around the house. Terry must get himself a paper route, Mom said. He's too young, he should enjoy his childhood, Dad said. He doesn't want to be a child, Mom said. But it might harm his grades, Dad said. Work never harmed any of us, Mom said. Or so I think they said, because they said it mostly in the German dialect they spoke when they did not want their younger children to understand them. For the first time, I felt a serious difference of opinion between them in which I played a leading role. You can have a paper route, but you must give it up if your marks begin to fall, my father said at the dinner table. That's where edicts were handed down.

My marks wouldn't suffer. After grades one and two, which were miserable because I was slow to learn what was being taught, and after much tutoring from my big sisters, school became a doddle. By the beginning of grade six and throughout grades seven and eight, I was spending half my days in the school library, getting my homework out of the way and then studying the history of the opening up of North America by Europeans, learning to recognize the stars from picture books, and reading my way through *The Posthumous Papers of the Pickwick Club,* through *Oliver Twist,* and deep into the collected works of Charles Dickens. I also followed Natty Bumppo through *The Last of the Mohicans* and the other Leatherstocking tales of James Fenimore Cooper. On Thursdays, as the school's projectionist, I showed National Film Board films all day long to one class after another. Even so, I either led my class or fell a close second to Brennan. Brennan, who shared library space with me, was interested in European political history. He prodded me to study the Russian Revolution and helped me formulate the kinds of questions about Red and White armies, Bolsheviks, Mensheviks, Leninists, and Trotskyites that my father gladly spent whole evenings answering. What had happened to my dyslexia?

If you can sound a word out, you can say it; if you can say it, you can see the word; if you can see the word, you can spell it, and once it is spelled, it is yours forever. That's the logic that defeats dyslexia. You sound a cluster of meaningless letters, one phoneme at a time, until you are saying a word; once it is said, you see it, you actually see it, and it stays in place long enough to be spelled out. If you start doing this before you are seven, you can read as well as anybody else. And if you develop a taste for wrestling with words, you can learn to read better than many. I was a wrestler, and what a coach and matchmaker I found in my third grade teacher, Mrs. Doherty.

I can visualize most of my teachers at Holy Rosary School, but it's only Mrs. Doherty's voice that I can still hear. She had been trained, I suppose, in the art of elocution; I seem to remember her providing formal recitations in the cathedral's basement auditorium at St. Patrick's Day festivities. What I do remember with far greater accuracy is the way she introduced herself to us: "I am not Misses Door Tea, nor am I Misses Dour Tee. I am Miss-us-Dah-her-ti. Repeat after me, Miss-us-Dah-her-ti, and try to get a hint of a *c* before the *h* on the Dah." We repeated this until we got it right as a class and individually. Mrs. Doherty drilled us on the proper pronunciation of our own names, the names of Regina's streets, Canada's provinces, Commonwealth countries, and the animals we might meet in the London Zoo. A tiger is a tiger is a tiger — never a tigger nor a tagger nor anything else any of our wayward lips, tongues, and mouths wanted to maul it into. We must have learned more than spelling and reading out loud to the rest of the class, but that's all I remember us doing hour after hour, day after day. Mrs. Doherty caught on right away to my trick of skipping words that gave me trouble, and she gave me my first dictionary, taught me how to use it to discover for myself how to pronounce words and find out their multiple meanings, and thanked me for every new word I brought her.

Delivering newspapers wasn't just an after school job and a source of steady income. It separated me further from my schoolmates, introduced me to boys who went to other schools, boys more ambitious than my classmates, who wanted to work to save money for university educations or guitars or hockey equipment or fast cars out of Regina, paper boys full of the ideas and projects that eventually turned them into lawyers and politicians and sports writers or long haul truck drivers or bar band singers or professional athletes or petty criminals. Hanging out with them at Woolworth's record bar on Saturday mornings, waiting for the early delivery of the weekend edition, I was moved by their talk into a much wider world of human possibility than that island I'd composed for myself.

Simon, who became an NDP Member of the Legislative Assembly, introduced me to my first paper route. That first route was not far from my home on Angus Crescent. It started at the top of my street but a block over, ran down Garnet Street from College Avenue to Wascana Creek, and took in blocks bounded by Garnet, Cameron, and Robinson Streets before turning back up to the terrace on 18th Avenue. It was a very mixed and muddy district. In 1955, the streets below 18th Avenue were gravelled, not paved, the sidewalks were boards, not concrete, and there were standpipes on the corners to provide water to a smattering of houses that lacked city services. Those same houses had outdoor toilets. Some of these humble dwellings were old (among them was a homesteader's shack), and others had been constructed in a hurry at the end of the war as "emergency shelters" on land that had been laid out as an adjunct to the Crescents but had not been built upon below 18th Avenue, except for a dozen or so houses as big as the developers had originally intended. It was a neigh-bourhood on the cusp of change; modern, low-slung ranch houses were going up, and one, unlike all others, was built of sheet glass and local field stones by an architect under the influence of Frank Lloyd Wright. During the year I delivered papers there, trenches were dug, mains and sewers were laid, sidewalks poured, roadways levelled and asphalted. Going door to door in the late afternoon with my papers and returning after dinner two nights a week to collect my money from those cus-tomers who generally sent me away empty-handed a couple of times before paying, I encountered people utterly unlike my own family and the families of my friends. In some houses there was cursing and shouting between husbands and wives, things getting broken, children crying. There were men who answered the door in their undershirts, women who had bruises that makeup didn't cover, and infants who ran to the door bare-assed and dirty-faced. "Uncles" moved in while the fathers were away. In two neighbouring houses of the poorest kind, husbands swapped wives and families in July and then swapped back again in September and left me wondering if I'd imagined it. At one house, a man who spoke with a French Canadian accent and sang with Hank Williams's Alabama drawl practised pedal steel guitar riffs and C&W vocal lines most days; he had a band of fiddles and guitars and drums in every Wednesday night to rehearse for weekend country dances. At other houses, men spent whole evenings and remarkable amounts of energy and disposable income in their garages, customizing hot rods or rebuilding motorcycles. My eyes opened wider and wider.

Much of that area was poorly lit, and some of it was dangerous because of the gangs of older teenage boys who passed through it on their way to and from the two footbridges that crossed Wascana Creek and opened conflicts between our neighbourhood and kids from Lakeview. I carried a powerful flashlight to guide my way and a policeman's whistle to frighten tormenters and summon help. I used the flashlight many times. I needed the whistle twice, and when it didn't work the second time, I armed myself with a taped roll of quarters to put power in my left fist. That was bravado; the boy who'd extorted money from me had slapped the whistle from my mouth and waved a switchblade knife. I knew who he was but wouldn't say because he was Hungarian, a recent refugee, I felt sorry for him, it was only a couple of dollars he took from me, it happened in my last month on that route, he'd frightened me half to death, and I was moving up to the Crescents with a larger, more lucrative, and safer route.

When my father was the age I then was, his world had altered much more dramatically. He was eleven when he arrived in Canada in 1913, the youngest child of homesteaders recruited by the Canadian Pacific

Railway. The old CP main line runs three blocks south of where I live. Westmount Station is closed now and awaiting gentrification, but in the year before the First World War began, it was a water stop for the train that bore my father and his family and thousands of others to the West as homesteaders. I sometimes find myself wondering if the boy who became my father looked out across open fields to the cluster of then-newly-built houses where I now live and wished that his journey was at an end and that he could settle in a house like my own. His parents were tailors who had little talent or taste for starting a farm where no farm had ever been. Canada needed homesteaders in the West, not more tailors in Montreal, and my grandparents needed the provisions of the Homestead Act to get into Canada. They were *Wolga-deutsch* from the town of Neu-Kolonie, and the Canadian government seemed benevolent.

Wolga-what? Some of us prefer to say *Volgadeutsch.* Either way, not many people get it right the first time. The Volgadeutsch occupied a German-speaking enclave in Russia; about half the size of Nova Scotia, it straddled the lower Volga between Saratov and Tsaritsyn (Volgo-grad). On August 12, 1939, Stalin and Hitler signed a non-aggression pact. As a result of this, Germans living in Bessarabia, Bukovina, Dobruja, Galicia, and Polish Volhynia were repatriated to Germany. When the Soviet Union went to war against Germany in 1941, Stalin denounced all German-speaking Russians as spies. Beginning on August 20, 1941, Germans living in areas not overrun by the German Army were deported to Siberia and the Asiatic Republics. The ethnic cleansing of the Volga Region took place in September 1941. How many were displaced? How many died? The Volga Germans are usually just lumped together with the approximately 1.2 million people of minor nationalities that Stalin suspected of treason — Kalmyks, Chechens, Ingushi, Karachai, Balkars, Tartars, Greeks, Bulgars, Armenians, Mesk-hetian Turks, Kurds, and Khemshins. They were women, children, and the elderly; the men had already gone into the army, and those who survived were sent into the gulag at the end of the war. They were dispossessed (Solzhenitsyn says that they were usually given one hour to pack) and transported, and the fatality rate was very high. In Martin Amis's meditation on Stalin and his legacy, *Koba the Dread: Laughter and the Twenty Million,* the Volga Germans take up barely two pages. But that wasn't altogether the end of them. The emigration of Germans from Russia to the Americas (of which my parents and grandparents were a part) had begun in the 1870s, when an exemption from military service was revoked and a policy of Russification was adopted amid growing hostility towards foreigners, particularly Germans. Volgadeutsch settled in Illinois, Nebraska, Kansas, the Dakotas, Saskatchewan, Alberta — regions that resembled areas they had left behind in Russia — and then spread into Colorado, Montana, Idaho, Washington, Oregon, British Columbia, California, Oklahoma, and Texas. Chile, Brazil, and Argentina took those whose poor health kept them out of North America. It's difficult to track who is related to whom among us. In the original settlement records, Russian officials recorded German names in the Cyrillic alphabet; the spoken dialect provides for variant spellings in both German and Russian; more changes occurred in English transliteration; and when individuals came into the United States and Canada, names were written as understood by the immigration official and frequently altered beyond recognition. To be a Rigelhof is also to be a Rigelhoff, a Riegelhof, a Ridelhof, a Riegel, a Riedel, a Riddel, and a Riddle.

During World War I and World War II there was animosity towards German immigrants and German-speaking immigrants throughout North America. Many states passed legislation restricting the use of the German language as a measure to curtail the influence of their German populations. Either forcibly or voluntarily, many German-speaking citizens restricted or concealed their Germanness. After World War II came the Cold War and the Red Menace. Although most of the German-Russian immigrants had entered this country before the Bolshevik Revolution and the implementation of Communism and had lost contact with all their European relatives, thanks to Stalin's deportations, the fact that we were from Russia was sufficient reason to hate us. Some families found it easier to conceal their origins or demonstrate their loyalty with anglicized first names rather than endure prejudice. Germans from Russia are mostly indistinguishable from the citizens of Garrison Keillor's Lake Woebegone — the slow-speaking, self-effacing, retiring and retired small-town parents of a legion of baby-boom big-city nurses, teachers, lawyers, doctors. The more famous include John Denver, Armin Mueller-Stahl, Angie Dickinson, Senator Tom Daschle, Lawrence Welk and his drummer, the pianist Svyatoslav Richter, Willard Schmidt, who pitched for the Cardinals and for the Reds during the 1950s and 1960s and once shared the single-game major league record for being hit the most times by pitchers, Alfred Kokh, who was elected as head of Russia's privatization agency in 1997 and became Deputy Prime Minister of Russia, a couple of astronauts, and maybe Tonya Harding, Cheryl Ladd, and, just maybe, Cary Grant, but definitely Lenin, yes, most definitely Lenin. Vladimir Ilyich's mother, Maria Alexandrovna Blank, was a Lutheran of Volga German heritage, and Vladimir Ilyich Ulyanov, *aka* Lenin, was born in the town of Simbirsk, later renamed Ulyanovsk, which is on the Volga River.

The original German colonists in Russia were allowed to maintain German language and culture in their own schools. Until the Russification policies came into force in the 1870s, two hundred years later, and settlers became increasingly exogamous, the colonists spoke primarily, oftentimes exclusively in German dialects that are distinct from those now spoken in Germany. My mother's father, John Behm, spoke Russian, served in the Russian Imperial Army, fought in the Russia-China war, and was decorated by the Tsar himself. As a soldier and a war hero, his word had carried weight in Neu-Kolonie when people pondered the future and wondered what would happen to them if

Russia went to war against Germany. Two years after he left for Canada with my grandmother and the toddler who was to become my mother, my father's family followed. The families were good friends and related to one another — two of my four great grandmothers were twin sisters.

It's doubtful that my father daydreamed about what has become the reality of my everyday life. If he was awake while the train took on water in Westmount, his eyes would more likely have been drawn to the large church in the neo-Byzantine basilica style being erected further up the hill that year by a wealthy congregation of Presbyterians. My father might have mistaken it for an Orthodox Christian place of worship, or even a Muslim one. He wouldn't have known what a Presbyterian was. But it's far more likely he was asleep. He must have been very tired by the time he reached Canada. It had been a long journey. Asleep, he might have been dreaming about the place from which he'd come. He knew it well and remembered it in detail to the end of his days. It was his first home, and he impressed upon me its history during the long walks we frequently took together.

Our ancestors were Hessians, and by the mid-eighteenth century Kassel and Darmstadt were among the most demoralized places in Europe. A century and a half of unending warfare, civil strife, excessive taxation and levies, enforced labour, military conscription, gang rapes, and religious rivalries left the living more than half-dead. The wars dislocated many people: the population of Hesse included refugees from Holland, Belgium, France, Austria, Switzerland, Luxembourg, Denmark, Hungary, Sweden, Italy, Scotland, and England. In 1762, at the end of the Seven Years' War, Catherine the Great opened Russia to all persons except Jews who wanted to settle there, and the displaced of Hesse started weighing the possibilities. When Catherine issued a second settlement manifesto on July 22, 1763, that offered religious and political autonomy, transportation, and land, my ancestors joined the line of migrants. They settled in the lower Volga on land dotted with the burial mounds of the Kirghiz, Turko-Tatar tribesmen descended from Genghis Khan's Golden Horde. In 1774, Kirghiz raiders destroyed two of the new settlements and abducted many female colonists, some of whom were returned physically and sexually battered after ransoms were paid. The survivors established a new Roman Catholic settlement — Neu-Kolonie, the birthplace of my father and my mother.

In German principalities, the religion of the prince determined the faith of his subjects. My father's family were Catholic dissenters from a Lutheran prince. The Russian government granted them religious freedom but not freedom from religion. Religious life was supported by governmental regulations: priests were forbidden to engage in any activities that were not specifically spiritual, and colonists were obliged to participate in religious worship with compulsory church attendance. The prohibition of all labour on Sundays or church holidays even forbade women to spin, knit, darn, or sew, and there were penalties for non-compliance. In this climate, Catholicism dominated intellectual and artistic life. Little was written down, much was memorized, and fine sermons were long remembered. A priest was a superior being, a priest could do no wrong.

There was a fundamental difference in temperament, a deep division in consciousness between my father and me. Even when I went walking with him, I still felt bound, chained like a Tatar raider who'd been captured by the more settled Germans. There was always a moral embedded in what my father said to me. He wanted me to think as he thought, and he thought living in the bosom of a large family within the embrace of the Catholic Church was the finest life a man could have or want to have. For him, freedom resided in obeying the voice of a Christian conscience formed by the teachings of the church. His world is as foreign to me now as my life in Westmount would have been to him then. There's a great deal about my father that I don't know at all, and much of what I do know I'm only now coming to understand as my life has passed the age his was when I knew him best. And not understanding Dad then, I didn't know how to please him, apart from devoting myself to his religion and listening attentively when he told me stories about his own childhood.

My father was the youngest in his family. Dad had a sister and four older brothers, and they all came to Canada, but not all at once and together. George, his oldest brother, left Russia in 1907, when he was eighteen and had completed his education. George travelled to England and then to Argentina and the United States, looking for the best place to settle. He came to Canada as a farm labourer and moved to Battleford, where he found work digging trenches for water mains and sewer pipes. He wrote back home about good land that was opening up in Alberta. My father and his brother Michael came out with their parents. Their sister Katie and her husband, Mike Ziegemann, came up from Argentina with their two daughters. Aunt Katie was three months pregnant with their son when a ditch Mike was digging for the city of Battleford collapsed, and he was killed. My two other uncles found their way to Battleford by circuitous routes, one of them going AWOL from the Russian army along the way. On July 23, 1913, Uncle George filed for a homestead on the northwest quarter of Section 33, Township 34, Range 1, west of the fourth meridian. My grandparents filed a homestead on the adjoining northeast quarter, five miles north and east of Altario, Alberta. They started out farming by breaking sod with a team of oxen and a walking plough. They bought horses as soon as they could. Not soon enough for his liking, my father said.

Horses. Their horses. That's what I always wanted to hear about, but the horses weren't what my father most wanted to talk about when he talked about his early years in Canada. His own horse had caught a hoof in a gopher hole and fallen on him. His horse broke its leg, and he had to shoot it. It really wasn't something he wanted to talk about, except as a cautionary tale about the pain and danger, the frustration and suffering of farm life. My father and three of his brothers before him all turned their backs on farming as soon as they could in favour of wholesale and retail trade, town and city life — only Uncle George stayed on the homestead. Uncle George's life and the lives of his wife and their nine children weren't the lives my father wanted for his own wife and children. For the first fifteen years, farming was good for Uncle George; he prospered, and the home farm expanded to a full section. When the Dirty Thirties brought drought, dust storms, and grasshoppers, the family couldn't survive on the little wheat and few potatoes they grew. To keep going, they needed the salt cod shipped from Newfoundland fishing villages, the white beans and apples from Ontario farms, and the seven dollars a month they got from the government to purchase flour, yeast, salt, sugar, coffee, and tea. In return for this relief money, Uncle George worked at building a road from Altario to Bodo. In 1937, there was no feed in the district, so cattle and horses were shipped south at government expense to Red Deer for the winter. In the spring, the government refused to pay return freight. Uncle George hitched a ride to Red Deer, sold his cattle, bought a saddle pony, and drove his horses back home. He was the closest thing to a cowboy that there ever was in our family. I loved that story. For me, it was full of adventure. My father had already had all the adventures he'd wanted to have by the time I was born. He was the child of another age, and he wanted my childhood to last longer than his own.

Every time the *Leader-Post* ran to more than fifty pages, carriers were given two movie passes to any Famous Players theatre as a bonus. The *Leader-Post* exceeded fifty pages at least once a week. If I went downtown on a Saturday morning and picked up my papers at the newspaper office around eleven-thirty, took the bus to my route, and worked quickly, I could be in a seat at the Capitol Theatre for the one-thirty showing. I loved movies. I loved adventure movies. The glory days of the cowboy film had passed, but there were still some fine westerns in 1956 and 1957 — John Wayne in *The Searchers,* James Stewart in *The Man from Laramie,* Audie Murphy in *Walk the Proud Land,* Gary Cooper in *Friendly Persuasion,* Burt Lancaster and Kirk Douglas as Wyatt Earp and Doc Holliday in *Gunfight at the OK Corral,* Elvis Presley in *Love Me Tender.*

My father and I did not see eye to eye on Elvis.

Elvis was getting into my hairdo.

Elvis was getting into my turned-up shirt collars and pegged trousers.

Elvis was getting into my lips.

Elvis was getting into the way I moved.

I was moving and grooving, slipping and sliding, splishing and splashing, rocking and rolling, twisting and shouting into my teens.

Then things really went out of control.

SEVEN

In the Middle of a Heartache

My father, Philip Rigelhof, died on January 7, 1958, in the morning, at home, in his own bed. Dad was three days short of his fifty-sixth birthday. He had started out walking to work at the provincial government building on Albert Street as he regularly did, but he'd felt unwell and come back to the house and gone to bed. At his request, both the doctor and the priest had been called. Father Walt arrived in time to administer Extreme Unction and hear my father's last breaths. A week earlier, our family doctor had told Dad he was perfectly fit, good for another thirty years. He died unexpectedly of a coronary thrombosis which was smoking-related and a medical mishap. These days it would be the subject of lawsuits, but people didn't think that way back then. Dad was a lifelong smoker, a heavy smoker who loved to blow smoke through his nose. He blew the lining out of his nostrils. He developed severe nosebleeds. Salves and ointments didn't prevent them. Sometimes he lost so much blood he needed transfusions. The doctor cauterized his nostrils. Dad kept smoking. He started bleeding again. The doctor treated him with a coagulating agent developed for hemophiliacs. We know now that it had been inadequately tested and caused thrombosis in too many cases — but that only became public knowledge years and years later.

That morning Dad and I ate breakfast together on our own. My older sister and brother were still on school holidays and were sleeping in, my mother and little sister had already consumed their breakfasts and were upstairs making beds and getting dressed for school. I didn't realize at first that their absences were arranged for my benefit. It was time for a heart-to-heart talk, father to son. It didn't go well. In the preceding eight months, I'd grown seven inches. I was almost as tall as my brother, my shoe size was edging close to my father's, my voice was deepening. Our confrontation was just a skirmish, a manchild and the aging head of the house locking horns. Since then, I've heard similar stories with minor variations from both fathers and sons many times over. I can laugh about it now, but ruefully.

We quarrelled that morning over my black leather jacket. Dad hadn't liked my buying a black leather jacket in the first place, but that wasn't the issue that day. The issue was, why hadn't I been wearing it? The issue was, why wasn't it in my clothes closet? The issue was, why was a certain girl in my grade eight class wearing it? The upshot: I'd better be wearing it when I came home. I left the kitchen table in a hurry, I rattled the glass in the front door as I slammed it. I knew I was going to be in trouble either with her or with him. I was a bit late coming home for lunch. Wearing both my leather jacket and my grey duffle coat, I was overdressed and steaming. As I came along the curve of Angus Crescent, it didn't register at first that there were many more cars parked along the street than was normal for a weekday morning. As I neared 209, I began to notice them. Then, yes, I saw that three of the cars belonged to my brothers-in-law, that another was Father Walt's, that another belonged to one of my uncles. I came up the front walk thinking something funny was going on but not thinking that it was anything bad. Father Walt opened the door for me. He said, "Terry, I'm sorry to tell you that your father died this morning. Go upstairs to your room until you're ready to come down."

As I stepped past people without seeing who they were, I wondered why I should go upstairs, and going up the stairs I wondered if maybe my father was lying dead in my bedroom and I was supposed to see him one last time and say a prayer for him, but Dad wasn't there, and I didn't see him when I looked in my parents' bedroom. He wasn't there or anywhere. But I did as I'd been told and went back into the bedroom I shared with my brother and sat on the bed and wondered what was going to happen next. Nothing did, until one of my brothers-in-law came in and handed me one of the black neckties and one of the black armbands he'd just bought downtown and said something sympathetic that I ignored and something practical about washing my face and changing into Sunday clothes and putting on that tie and armband and coming downstairs as soon as I felt I could and sitting with my mother. I remember telling him that I had nothing to wear that the black tie went with, and I don't think this was really a fashion statement, although it sounded an awful lot like one. I think I meant that I felt naked. A child does not experience death for the first time the way that an adult experiences death for the first time, except in this: in our panic, each of us focuses on some minor detail, me on what shirt to wear with that black tie and armband. And my brother-in-law said, "A white shirt goes with any tie."

When I removed my school clothes, I noticed that I had one of those tremendous, awkward, absolutely rigid erections adolescent boys get, but for once it didn't feel urgent or embarrassing. It was just there, and then as I sat looking at it, it deflated. And so did everything else. The air just went out of everything, and everything seemed to be swallowed up by blackness, as if I was going to pass out. That didn't happen either. I have no words of my own for what did happen, but Virginia Woolf, who lost her mother at the very same age, wrote in "Reminiscences" that "it was as though on some brilliant day of spring the racing clouds of a sudden stood still, grew dark, and masked themselves; the wind flagged, and all creatures on the earth moaned or wandered seeking aimlessly." When I read this, I recognized it.

There was much crying and comforting going on as I came back downstairs. I'd shaved even though there was little to shave, I'd styled my hair a little less Elvis-y, and I'd dressed up in black slacks, white shirt, and new black tie. Not knowing which sleeve I was to wear it on or how to pin it to my shirt, I carried my armband until it was pinned on me by I don't remember whom, because our house was jammed with people. Sisters, brother, brothers-in-law, aunts, uncles, friends, neighbours, priests crammed every corner of every room, but none of them nor any of their voices felt real or human or approachable. It felt as if all of them were dead and ghosts and I alone was alive, and I remember thinking that as I'd walked home from school what must really have happened was that Russia and America started waging World War III, A-bombs had gone off, the entire world had been nuked, and, unaccountably, I was the sole survivor in my family and neighbourhood. I felt I needed to get out of the house and retrace my steps to the schoolyard and find another survivor somewhere. I remember hoping it would be that girl who had just given me back my black leather jacket. I couldn't get near the front door and that jacket. I couldn't leave the house. Like Charlie Chaplin's waiter who can't get off the dance floor and unload his tray in *Modern Times*, I kept being pushed into the middle of throngs. Those ghosts kept putting arms around my shoulders or holding my hands and telling me things, but no one could tell me why I should have been the last to know my father had died. The principal of my school had been phoned, and someone in the family had come and taken my little sister home right away, but the principal thought it best that the grade eight class not be disturbed by my early exit. I was left oblivious to walk home alone and be the last to know, expected to adjust in a moment to what everyone else had known and absorbed for at least an hour. At that moment and for years afterwards, that hour's difference made me feel completely different, completely shut out from whatever it was the other members of the family experienced.

To me, then, in those few minutes, not only the world changed but I changed. I was more alone than Robinson Crusoe, I was once again Paul Savard, but I didn't have a horse to my name. I was too old to ride radiators, and it was too cold and the streets were too slippery with packed snow to ride my bicycle. I was a solo traveller and immobilized; I had to find some way to live on my own in the world. And I thought of Paul Savard and the chapters in *Painted Arrows* when his mare Flash sprains her ankle and Paul digs a cave beside a creek and masks it with branches. Paul gets sick, but he finds the courage and strength to nurse and protect himself and his horse and bring them both back to health. My family was crying and talking to one another and nursing and protecting one another, but I wasn't able to do any of those things. They were in the living room or the dining room. These two rooms had been at the centre of my father's world. He loved to talk, and he loved to have his family and friends share a meal with him. He had also spent more time in the kitchen than most fathers of that era. Dad was an enthusiastic washer of dishes and scrubber of pots and pans, but even so the kitchen was Mom's and the place where I felt most comfortable, outside my bedroom, with its books, or the attic with its little telescope and large view of the night sky.

A lifetime of reading books and, as an adult, teaching young adults has taught me that I was far from alone in feeling so utterly alone. For a child, a loved one's death is an unshared experience, a catastrophe, something so disconnected from the expected that there are no words for it nor even, in my case, tears. Paul Savard wept and then did what had to be done. I had no tears and didn't know quite what to do. I wanted it to be midnight and the house empty and myself in the attic alone with the stars, but it wasn't and wouldn't be for hours if ever again, so I went to the kitchen, and my mother wasn't there but her friends were, and food was being prepared, and I had an enormous emptiness that needed to be filled with an urgency that surpassed normal appetite or Sunday table manners. I started to eat, and oh how those good women wanted to feed me. I ate, and sometimes, in retrospect, it seems to me that I ate for days without stopping. Food kept coming through our front and back doors for weeks on end, as my mother's many friends made certain that she didn't have meals to worry about until long after the funeral was over, visitors stopped popping in at all hours, and our lives fell back into some more regular pattern. I know I ate and ate and ate. And grew.

I know I grew another four inches between my father's death and my birthday late in April.

I don't know how many pounds I packed on, but I know I weighed 149 pounds on my birthday and stood five feet eleven inches tall.

I know that I outgrew everything in my closet and that much of what was needed to replace shirts, sweaters, and jackets with sleeves that no longer met my wrists and trousers with legs that no longer covered my ankles came to me only slightly used from a family up the street, whose only son was four years and a couple of steps ahead of me in his own growth spurts. But that knowledge followed experience, and my experience was of eating and eating and never feeling the hunger go away. That was afterwards. In the middle of all those grieving people, I did not know how to grieve as they did. The reason was inexperience. Of the people in those rooms, only my little sister was less experienced in the facts of death than I was. My father's parents had lived the last years of their lives with us on Angus Crescent — Grandpa Rigelhof died on December 6, 1946, when I was two-and-a-half, Grandma Rigelhof died on March 14, 1948, when I was not yet four. My Grandpa Behm died when I was less than five months old, on September 22, 1944, predeceased by Grandma Behm on November 8, 1939. I sometimes think I remember Grandpa Rigelhof's being taken from the house on a stretcher and never returning, but I think what I am really remembering is what others have remembered of my behaviour towards him. I do remember Grandma in her final illness in her bedroom, but I do not remember her dying. My brother and sisters did, and the older ones remembered all the other deaths.

Only connect. "Only connect! . . . Live in fragments no longer. Only connect, and the beast and the monk, robbed of the isolation that is life to either, will die," E.M. Forster writes in *Howard's End*. Only connect.

People who study these things professionally say that humans form attachments to other humans as instinctively as we feed or mate. The pioneer in this field was Mary D. Salter Ainsworth, who got her start in psychology at the University of Toronto and found early confirmation for her theory of attachment during her stint in the Canadian Women's Army Corps during World War II. In 1978, she and her colleagues published the book on the subject, *Patterns of Attachment: A Psychological Study of the Strange Situation*. They show that an infant's primary needs are touch, eye contact, movement, smiles, and nourishment. Through these interactions, a child learns that the world is a safe place and develops trust. Through these interactions, a child's brain develops to its optimum, and physiological, cognitive, emotional, and social health is established. So say the experts, and it sounds right to the rest of us. They also say that impairment and disorder of these interactions through domestic violence, substance abuse, sexual interference, death, and other pathologies alter a child's behaviour in some or all of the following ways: increase of superficial charm; decrease of genuine affection; preoccupation with fire, blood, gore, violent death; aggression towards others manifested by controlling, bossy, manipulative, defiant, argumentative, demanding, impulsive actions; aggression against the self manifested by destructive, accident-inducing activities; rages and temper tantrums in response to adult authority; poor eye contact, except when lying; compulsive lying; lack of self-control; lack of cause-and-effect thinking; compulsive stealing; defiance; lack of remorse; lack of conscience; difficulty maintaining friendships; persistent nonsense questions; incessant chatter; grandiosity in sense of self; lack of trust in others to provide care and attention.

Only connect.

Only connect, and the bestial boy and the monkish manchild, robbed of the isolation that is life to either, will die with all their superficial charms, preoccupations, aggressions, compulsions, defiance, nonsense, chatter, grandiosity.

Only connect.

Only I didn't.

The only people I felt more rather than less attached to in the days of mourning and the months that followed were the little girl who understood even less of death than I did, my younger sister, and our mother. And attachment to them and their good opinion of me led me to become less of a bestial boy and less of a monkish manchild than I might have otherwise become, but I was tempted, tempted, tempted.

I didn't connect any longer with those who had been my friends.

I didn't connect any longer with most of the movies I'd been seeing.

I didn't connect any longer with many of the books I'd been reading.

I started reading Shell Scott and Mickey Spillane mysteries and the sexually educative bestseller *Peyton Place.*

I watched the oldest movies I could find on television or, occasionally, at the easternmost of Regina's movie theatres, the Roxy, on 12th Avenue between Broad and Osler Streets. The Roxy had been converted from an automobile showroom in the 1930s, and by the late fifties catered to a mixed daytime clientele of pensioners, the unemployed, shift workers, and fine arts students from Regina College. They nodded through or revelled in cheap double or triple bills which sometimes included Charlie Chaplin or Buster Keaton silent films alongside the mild porn of Steve Reeves romping with the vestal virgins of ancient Rome or Greece. And, miracle of miracles, sometime in the weeks following my father's death, on a day when I couldn't face school, Albert Lewin's production of Oscar Wilde's *The Picture of Dorian*

Gray, with Hurd Hatfield, George Sanders, Donna Reed, Angela Lansbury, and Peter Lawford, on a double bill with Michael Redgrave, Edith Evans, Joan Greenwood, and Margaret Rutherford in Anthony Asquith's production of Wilde's *The Importance of Being Earnest*. Instantly, I became a rabid Wilde fan and borrowed his books from the Regina Public Library. In his novel, Wilde says that Dorian, while thinking of the greatest writers and painters, concludes "that in some mysterious way their lives had been his own" and that literary ancestors might be "nearer in type and temperament, many of them, and certainly with an influence of which one was more absolutely conscious" than one's own living relations. What a thought! My true family of kindred types and temperaments was hanging on the walls of the Norman McKenzie Art Gallery or lodged on library shelves. And what a gift his wordplay was!

One-sided mock-Wildean wordplay in the schoolyard led to fistfights with classmates, and an exchange of wild punches and mild profanities with one of them in the Cathedral basement after an evening service led to my expulsion from the altar boys society.

I was happy to leave. I didn't like the priest who had been put in charge after Father Walt was promoted to more important duties in the parish. I didn't like the meetings he called and required us to attend, the floor hockey and shuffleboard games he organized, the Bing Crosby, Pat O'Brien, and Spencer Tracey movies he showed in the cathedral basement, the talks he gave us about having faith in God, respecting our parents, loving our siblings, obeying our teachers, and believing that our prayers would be answered so long as we prayed for the things that were truly good for us, things such as doing our best on school tests. I hated his dumb jokes, and I hated the bear hugs he gave us and the pats on the back that made me cringe. I did not want to be touched, even casually and innocently, by any man.

I'd served alongside Father Walt at my father's funeral without breaking into tears. It was duty enough. It was more than enough altar boy duty. Roman Catholicism had been my father's world: Dad had been a hundred per cent Roman Catholic, and there were people who sincerely called him a saint and others who said he was more Catholic than the Pope. After he died, I wanted as little to do with his religion as I could manage without upsetting my mother too much. I didn't tell Mom about the fistfight and expulsion. I told her I was too busy with my paper route to attend all the meetings and rehearsals that were required of altar boys. Money was short. Dad had left us with a small pension, a mortgage, no life insurance. Mom had to find work. My paper route came first. And then, soon after, I started a second job at a florist's shop and found rituals that were more to my liking.

EIGHT

Saturday's Child

Monday's child is fair of face,
Tuesday's child is full of grace,
Wednesday's child is full of woe,
Thursday's child has far to go,
Friday's child is loving and giving,
Saturday's child works hard for a living,
But the child that is born on the Sabbath Day
Is bonny and blithe and good and gay!

I've spent far too much of my life thinking of myself as a Saturday's child and acting like one.

In fact, I'm one of the "fair of face" — a Monday's Child, the day of my birth remembered in family lore as the day that the clothesline blew down in an April gust, and the bedding got a mud bath, and the washing got done a second time that day with the help of a kindly next-door neighbour and a warm evening breeze.

Clotheslines! Monday washday! Backyards up and down street after street with washing pegged out to dry in the breeze through every

Monday morning of the year except the very coldest. Who, under fifty, remembers wringer washing machines and clotheslines filled with Monday's washing? Or clothes pegs? On our side of the street in Westmount, only the single mom across the back from us regularly hangs laundry out on a clothesline. She's years younger than me, a nurse, a long-ago immigrant from England. Like ourselves, everyone else uses automatic washers and tumble dryers and puts in a load whenever the hamper is full. Mondays are no more washday than Sundays are the old, heavily regulated Lord's Day: a day for going to church in best clothes to be preached at about the evils of going to movies on Sundays, watching Sunday night television, or, horror of horrors, attending Saturday dances that did not end at a quarter to midnight, and then everyone but mothers spending much of the day "at rest," reading what was good for our souls until company arrived for Sunday dinner. In 1958, only a few households on the Crescents had automatic washers and tumble dryers, about as many as had a freezer chest in the basement, a second television set, or a high-fidelity record player. Or two telephones. Nearly everybody went to church on Sunday, almost every Sunday. On Angus Crescent, the exceptions were few and noticeable. This was the era of the newly standardized five-day, forty-hour work week. Government services closed on Saturdays and Sundays. Shops closed Sundays and Mondays and stayed open two nights a week until nine o'clock only during the Christmas shopping season. This was the era when the few married women who worked outside the home were mostly nurses or teachers.

At the beginning of this new century, more than a generation later, eight out of ten Canadians still identify themselves as Christians. Roman Catholics make up 45% of the population, Protestants 33%, according to Statistics Canada. People of all other religions or no religion account for the remaining 22%. But what is true for the nation as a whole is not true of any one region. Quebec is still predominantly Roman Catholic (83%), but in the West, Catholics make up a quarter of the population, with Saskatchewan at 29%. Roughly half of the populations of provinces other than Quebec are Protestant, ranging from 54% in Saskatchewan to 42% in Ontario. East of Quebec, the number of people who are neither Roman Catholic nor Protestant is statistically negligible. In Saskatchewan, they account for 3%, in Quebec approximately 4%, and in Ontario 8% of the total population. Sixteen percent of Canadians, including me, say we have no religion. This group, which has been growing steadily since the 1950s, is largest in British Columbia at more than 30% and smallest (nearly none) in Newfoundland, Prince Edward Island, and New Brunswick. Two per cent of Canadians identify themselves as Muslim and one per cent each as followers of Judaism, Buddhism, Hinduism, or Sikhism.

There is, of course, a large and important distinction between identifying your religious affiliation and observing the practices of your religion. Or assenting to its beliefs. At the beginning of the new millennium, about one in three of the Canadian adults who declare a religious affiliation admit that they do not attend religious services at all. Back in the fifties, more than two out of three respondents to a Gallup poll had attended a religious service in the previous week. By 2003, fewer than one in five had done so, and those who did attend were disproportionately new immigrants. All this suggests to me to that most of us born in Canada, not wishing to forsake the faith of our ancestors, continue claiming membership in a religion we rarely practice and adherence to a creed we no longer believe. Christianity is most comfortable to the majority of Canadians as an element of folklore that can be fallen back upon whenever births, marriages, and deaths demand larger buildings and more elements of ritual than secular observances can provide. When Canadians are asked if they're Catholic and answer in the affirmative, they don't mean that they personally profess what their church teaches. By the standards of Pope John Paul II and his curia, the majority of Canadian Catholics are schismatic. According to various polls, more than 90% of Canadian Catholics approve of contraception, more than 80% approve of sex outside marriage and are willing to accept both married and female clergy, more than 50% find homosexuality morally acceptable, and over 35% accept abortion — all of which are contrary to the explicit teachings of John Paul II's Vatican. It's a position that I don't share but one I do think I understand: some people need more in the way of costumes, ceremonies, and rituals and less in the way of logical coherence in their religious beliefs than others, especially when it comes to the great mysteries of birth, marriage, and death. In Quebec, for instance, regular church attendance among baptized Catholics dropped from 88% in 1965 to well under 20% in 2003, and churches would be very empty without immigrants from Latin America to bulk up the numbers. Quebec's Catholics are also more tolerant on sexual and reproductive issues than their co-religionists elsewhere across the country, as are their clergy. The church in Quebec openly challenges regulations laid down in Rome, dispensing sacraments to the divorced, baptizing the offspring of the unmarried, marrying or burying such former communicants as Celine Dion, René Levesque, Pierre Elliot Trudeau, and even the long-time public atheist Pierre Bourgeault, and allowing eulogies to be delivered inside the church. The most surprising aspect of this permissiveness is that no one seems surprised by it any more.

In Regina in my youth, people were surprised when they no longer saw me serving at the altar. People were surprised when my mother found a way of supporting herself and her four youngest children without leaving the house by making herself over into a professional dressmaker and seamstress. With six daughters, my mother was used to making things over, altering and adjusting clothes to fit growing bodies and changing styles. She was very good at it, too, so accomplished that she was soon specializing in bridal gowns and bridesmaids' dresses. My brother helped out by selling men's clothing and my older sister by working in a drugstore on Saturdays. And then, to my own surprise, I too became a Saturday's child.

In 1958, March 15, the Ides of March, fell on a Saturday. It was my first Saturday working at Frank Markham's Flowers on Hamilton Street. I remember it because it was St. Patrick's Day weekend and the greenest day in my life. Frank Markham no longer owned the business, although he dropped by his old shop that day and most Saturdays I worked there, just to say hello to the women who'd once worked for him and to touch the fresh flowers and have a small rose pinned to his lapel. The new owner spent little time in this store because he owned another a couple of blocks away that carried his own name. I should name that name because I owe him a great debt of gratitude, but I don't know if Leslie (to call him by a name I never used) would like to be remembered for doing what he did for me and what he didn't do. He hired me even though he didn't know me or my family. He simply took the word of a friend of my father's that I was a good, reliable boy who learned quickly and was willing to work hard. And he didn't fire me when he discovered that I'd lied about my age — I was a month short of fourteen rather than sixteen when I began working for him. At the start, he'd been willing to pay me out of petty cash and to wait a month for me to show up with an Unemployment Insurance book. I kept him waiting more than two years, and then, the day I turned sixteen, I quit working for him. He understood. I had a better job waiting for me. There were no hard feelings; I ended my employment with Leslie as I'd begun it by working as hard as I could as best I could doing anything and everything that was asked of me for as many hours as he needed me.

That first Saturday at the florist's and every Saturday after that until I gave up my paper route six months later, I followed the same routine — a routine more satisfying to me than any Mass I'd ever served. Arriving at work at eight o'clock, I swept out the premises from front to back, cleaned and swept the sidewalk in front of the shop, squeegeed the store's plate glass front door and display windows outside and inside, wiped away fingerprints and polished the fronts of the refrigerated cases where the cut flowers were kept, changed the water in all the containers of cut flowers, then watered dozens and dozens of potted plants, until the women who served the customers at the front of the shop and filled the orders at the back wanted to break for coffee. I took their orders and went up the street to the LaSalle Hotel with some flowers for the cashier and brought back deeply discounted coffees, teas, and pastries. After the break, I ran errands between Leslie's two shops and made small deliveries in the immediate area till twelve noon, when I crossed the street to the *Leader-Post* building, picked up two big bags of papers, hopped the bus, ran my route, stopped at home for a very fast lunch, hopped the bus back downtown, and spent the next three hours learning as much as I could about cutting and arranging flowers, caring for plants, and serving customers. I made myself useful during the final hour by cleaning up the shop and closing it down for Tuesday's re-opening.

I loved every minute of it. I loved the anonymity of being a boy with a broom or a mop and bucket cleaning floors or a delivery kid in jeans and a leather jacket with a parcel under my arm, scurrying through finely dressed crowds of Saturday shoppers and a parade of window shoppers. I loved getting to know downtown people by name, gathering insider knowledge, being able to enter shops through their back doors. I loved being an observer who went about his business unobserved because people buying flowers always had their minds on other things — wonderful things like births and birthdays, big formal dances, weddings and wedding anniversaries, romances. Or dreadful things like funerals and the end of affairs. Or merely rueful things like wild, wicked flings. The deliveries I savoured were the bouquets of roses I carried to young and no-longer-so-young women at the Georgia Hotel. The Georgia was the newest of the downtown hotels and the only one where I was allowed to take flowers up to the rooms rather than leave them at the front desk. And I knocked on doors that opened to more lingerie and exposed flesh than I had ever seen in a house full of sisters.

I liked what I did and the things I saw even more when I stopped delivering newspapers and started spending Saturday mornings going out to churches in the delivery van and helping the driver set up the flower arrangements for weddings. It was deeply thrilling — I risked telling nobody about it — to actually enter the churches of other faiths. Catholics were forbidden under pain of sin to go inside non-Catholic places of worship. But I did and never bothered confessing it. I walked forbidden aisles and stepped inside heretical communion rails and carried flowers to the altars of all the downtown churches — St. Paul's Anglican Cathedral, Knox United, Metropolitan Methodist, First Baptist — and the outlying Carmichael United and Trinity Lutheran, and new ones like Grace Lutheran, and a cluster of smaller churches that belonged to groups I had never heard of.

I worked harder at that job than I've ever worked at anything in my life — and longer hours, too. Regina was mad for cut flowers and potted plants in those years, and the suppliers were few. For the major occasions of the year — Easter, Mother's Day, graduation dances, June weddings, and especially Christmas, with its holly, mistletoe, garlands, poinsettia, and Leslie's cunning indoor Christmas tree lot in an unheated building opposite the train station — there was so much to be done that I worked days so long they stretched past midnight, and I was sent home in a taxi at the boss's expense. I worked whenever I could at the florist's and cut lawns, watered gardens, or shovelled snow until I was old enough to take over from my brother at Simpson's. My only regret is that much too much of the giddy amount of money I earned was expended paying my way through Campion College, a private high school run by the Jesuit Fathers, and in consoling myself for its miseries with binge eating and drinking and then paying for prescribed medications to cure the cures for what ailed me. In what I still regard as the single greatest misfortune of my youth apart from losing my father, I was awarded a first year scholarship to Campion at my grade eight graduation. I hadn't earned it and I didn't want it. It was supposed to go to the boy with the highest average, and that was Brennan, but he, at his father's urging, declined it in my favour. It was no favour. I wanted a downtown high school to go with my downtown working life. I wanted to go to Central Collegiate. It was a shorter walk, it was co-ed and resolutely secular, no one else in my family had attended it, and it was a better school in the subjects I most wanted to study — literature, history, fine arts. But Father Walt told me to tell my mother that I would be allowed to attend with the church's permission only if I attended catechism classes at the Cathedral on Saturday mornings. I didn't want to go to Campion, but I didn't want to give up my Saturday job either. It seemed less of a struggle to do the unsurprising thing and go to the Jesuit school my brother had just graduated from, especially after I "won" the first year's tuition.

Central Collegiate is no more. It opened its doors in 1908 and closed them in June 1985. The fine building was demolished in 1994, although the facade was saved and rebuilt as the entrance to a new suburban high school. I walked by Central hundreds of times on my way home from my downtown jobs, but, after once seeing its fine arts room and what I would forever be missing, I only ever entered to attend basketball games and dances in its gymnasium. Campion College became my school, and it was a very different place. It had no room for fine arts and too much space for its own history and self-promoting propaganda. Campion had opened in 1918 with six students in two rented houses directly across the street from Holy Rosary Cathedral, and it moved in 1921 to a new three-storey building on 23rd Avenue and Albert Street, then on the outskirts of town. A wing was added in 1947 and a gymnasium in 1957. The buildings still exist but have been recycled, and Campion College still exists, but it's now located on the campus of the University of Regina and gave up teaching high-school boys years ago. These days, Campion is a small liberal arts college serving thirteen hundred students, and from all reports it does a good job of providing traditional education via a handful of Jesuits and a largely lay faculty. In 1962, the year I graduated from the high-school, a staff of twenty-one Jesuits and eight laymen taught three hundred and eighty-some students divided into four grades and three academic streams. There were also forty-eight first year Arts students, of whom fourteen were young women. Except in the C stream, in which commercial subjects replaced academic ones, the classes were large — just under forty students.

The A and B streams were rigorously segregated and intermingled only for French or German classes, and the high-school boys only occasionally caught sight of the young women in the co-ed Arts program. The major division that cut through the school, however, was between boarders and day scholars. There were always a few boarders from faraway Mexico and other Latin American countries and small clusters from Calgary and Edmonton, but most came from farms and small communities in rural Saskatchewan and Alberta. Campion earned its reputation as a first-rate boarding school in the thirties and forties by turning farm boys into professional men — teachers, lawyers, doctors, priests, and soldiers. I haven't carried many relics of my Saskatchewan youth into my Montreal maturity, but I do have the volumes of *The Campion*, the college yearbook, corresponding to my years there. The preface of the 1962 edition, the yearbook of my graduating class, says, "Over one thousand of its former students answered the call to arms in World War II, of whom forty gave their lives in their country's service." Among the Campion alumni, it cites with pride "eighty-eight priests, including Bishop Klein, D.D. of Saskatoon, and Abbott Weber, O.S.B.," the chief monk of the Benedictine Abbey at Muenster, Saskatchewan. A little later, in "A Letter from Fr. P.J. Boyle, S.J.," the principal of the day writes:

I can assure you that the Jesuit and lay faculty are men dedicated to your spiritual and academic progress. On your part, we expect dedication to your responsibilities as a student.

In a society where the mediocre and the second-rate is frequently the standard, I urge you to strive for academic excellence. Whatever your abilities may be, we expect your maximum.

In a generation, too, when churchmen, national leaders and educators decry the softness of the age, conformity to school regulations and discipline will develop in you a self-discipline that is spontaneous and voluntary. Here rests the basis of character.

Elsewhere, *The Campion* announced the "Theme" of our year:

Let us this year resolve to strive for
> PERFECTION

in our
> SPIRITUAL LIFE

that we may be always in a State of Grace and that we show unbounded love and Charity to our neighbour;
> ACADEMIC WORK

that we utilize our God-given talent to the best of our individual ability;
> GAMES AND EXTRA-CURRICULAR WORK

that develop our physical gifts from God to lead a healthy life and that we develop a catholic outlook.

The Jesuits liked to boast that if they were given a boy, they'd have the man for the rest of his life. I tried to make certain that wasn't going to happen to me.

NINE

Thomas Merton and Me

Dawson College, where I have taught since 1973, is a community college of a kind unique to Quebec. Most students enter at seventeen, the perfect age to get away from high school and start fresh on something new — a two-year pre-university program or a three-year program in a technology such as graphics, computers, design, nursing, photography, or professional theatre. It's a system of schooling that I like a lot. At their age, I was facing grade twelve, and my only options seemed to be stepping backwards into my father's Roman Catholic world or screwing up my life forever and forever amen. I thought I was doing a pretty good job of screwing up my life.

I had a big problem with girls and a bigger problem with my mouth. My problem with girls was that I couldn't connect with them in mutually satisfactory ways. I think I frightened them. I know I frightened myself. Part of my problem with girls and most of my problems with the rest of the world came from my mouth, my *big* mouth. I had something to say about everything, couldn't shut up about anything, and said it all quite impressively. My verbosity was superdeligorgeous. My words could be clever, biting, cynical, ironical. They were generally excessive, angry, sour, sarcastic, destructive, exhibitionistic, violent, and rudely honest, my way of thumbing my nose at a world that treated me badly and that I wanted to treat worse. So was smoking too much, listening to Miles Davis for hours on end, and drinking beer or hard liquor whenever and wherever I could and always to excess. I don't want to overdraw that self-portrait: I think I was also capable of being gentle, generous, sentimental, and shy — unexpectedly and usually at inappropriate moments. I fell in love about once every three weeks with different girls, whom of course I kept ignorant of the fact in the firm conviction that whomever I wanted to kiss could not possibly want me and my acne-riddled face kissing her. It was about the only matter on which I kept my mouth firmly shut. Unlike my friends with bigger dicks and smaller dictionaries, I never carried a safe in my wallet. It would have seemed too optimistic. Despite this, there were long evenings of conversation on front porches and in kitchens that were among the best hours of my adolescence. We did not know then what feminism was, but we did know that something was passing between us and altering our perceptions of one another in an egalitarian way that those older than we were didn't seem to experience.

What I remember best of those worst days of my life is the psychological abuse and fear-mongering that passed itself off as spiritual counselling at Campion, the Friday afternoon talks in the college chapel delivered by a bantamweight Jimmy Cagney-like former chaplain of Kingston Penitentiary. His idea of effective birth control was to fill the heads of schoolboys with stories of men he'd seen die so young and so horribly as to plunge their mothers into madness: "And let me tell you, mister, I saw that boy's mother go into complete catatonic shock from which she's never recovered when the cops handed her his blood-soaked personal effects and she saw the opened three-pack of Sheiks with one missing. It was in his wallet next to her picture. Mister, think of that the next time you get all dreamy-eyed reading poetry with some poor sweet innocent girl and think of putting your hand someplace it shouldn't go and a rubber on your pisser." One of the young women, a

Central Collegiate student with whom I spent some of the finest of those evenings, said, "I don't know why your teachers call themselves members of the Society of Jesus. It should be the Society of Zeus. They should call themselves Zeusites, not Jesuits. It's Zeus who lays it down as law that man must suffer into wisdom!" At Central, she got to study Homer and Aeschylus. I was stuck with Virgil's *Aeneid* and Cicero's speeches, translated and parsed ever so painfully as we were taught much of the grammar and little of the genius of classical Latin writers.

There wasn't much pleasure to be found in reading anything in that school. I found what pleased me in the avant-garde Modern Times Book Shop that Kerry and Helene (it was the sort of place where everybody was a regular and nobody seemed to know anybody's last name) had opened at 2439 11th Avenue, just a block or so west of the Grand Theatre. That's how I discovered it — going to the movies rather than to school. I first heard Ornette Coleman's *This Is Our Music* while reading Jack Kerouac's *On the Road* there. It was that kind of place, a store that grouped books by publisher not author, where there was a special shelf for books from New Directions, a company that published just about every poet who was anybody among the Beats and also, to my astonishment, Thomas Merton.

Thomas Merton was such a powerful writer to such a diversity of readers for so long that it's difficult to accept the fact that he's now more remembered than read. But in the two decades between the publication of his autobiography *The Seven Storey Mountain* in 1948 and his death on December 10, 1968, Merton became arguably the most famous Catholic priest in America and then the most controversial monk in the world. Merton was a poet, essayist, artist, activist, contemplative explorer of silence, reformer of monastic life, photographer, correspondent with many, confessor to some, bridge between Western and Eastern religious traditions, and something else besides — a sign of peace in troubled times. For some, such as George Woodcock, who was sometimes an atheist and always at least an agnostic, Merton was an influence who ranked alongside Tolstoy.

My own first contact with any of Merton's books came when the brother-in-law who had distributed the black ties and armbands on my father's day of death gave me a copy of *The Seven Storey Mountain* as a grade eight graduation present because I'd expressed some interest in becoming a writer, and Thomas Merton was his idea of the sort of writer I ought to become. I slotted the book into my bedroom bookshelf as soon as I worked out that it was the autobiography of a free-spirited Greenwich Village cartoonist and poet who'd become a priest. Cartoons and poems were things I admired; priests weren't, not just then. Not until I was seventeen and had some hard-won confidence in my ability to judge writers for myself did I actually read what Merton wrote. I read Merton's poems, and I was attracted to them and to him, but not enough to read *The Seven Storey Mountain.* I figured it had some connection to Dante's seven levels of purgatory, and my life had devils enough. I was on my way to hell in a hurry.

Or so the one Jesuit at Campion who seemed to care about me kept saying. He had a point. I was drinking heavily and not holding it well. Getting falling-down goofy every Friday and Saturday night and occasional Sunday afternoons was the best way I knew to keep from blowing up and getting expelled or arrested. The teacher trying to point my life in another direction was a priest with more credibility than most of the others: he actually seemed to like teaching us. He said all my anger and resentment and drinking was God's way of telling me that I had a vocation to the priesthood, maybe even to the Society of Jesus. He wanted to know what I thought of them. He told me he wasn't trying to recruit me, that Jesuits don't exert pressure, that he was just there to answer my questions and trusted in the Lord to do the rest. Christ is the answer, but you have to ask the question, he said. Jesus moves in mysterious ways. Didn't I have any questions at all?

I had one, but I didn't know exactly how to word it. He kept up the pressure that he said wasn't pressure until I finally asked, "If Jesuits are supposed to be the best priests in the world, why do you let bad teachers teach here?"

He lectured me on the philosophy of education practised by the Society of Jesus. I listened, and all the while I wondered how I could get him to understand that by *bad* I meant *sexually abusive*. It was difficult to say, even if at that time I had known the phrase. In clinical terms I hadn't been penetrated, just fondled. I hadn't been seduced, just propositioned. But it had happened in my very first week at that school with my homeroom teacher: a rub on the neck, a hand on the inside of the thigh, an unmistakable and horrifying offer of special friendship if I'd visit him in his room outside class hours. After I'd rejected him, he made sure that I never had any pleasure in any of his classes, even when we were reading Shakespeare. He made me suffer every agony within his power to inflict, and he frustrated my attempts to learn anything by undermining my self-confidence. What made the bullying worse, far worse, was the way he made me feel that I was at fault every time anything went wrong in class. So when the priest who had only my best interests at heart ended his lecture and waited for me to say something, I just blurted out, "I didn't mean bad as in pedagogy, I meant bad as in pederasty."

He told me I'd used a word I didn't understand.

I said I didn't think so. I told him about the fondling I'd experienced and its repercussions.

He told me I was being untruthful and deliberately offensive and asked me to get down on my knees and apologize and say an Act of Contrition.

I didn't. It was a Friday, and I stormed off before I got sick all over his shoes. I then got enormously drunk on rum at the school's football game. By Monday, I was sick enough to stay home until the family doctor put me in hospital for three weeks so that I could be given two penicillin injections in the butt three times a day for a severe kidney infection. The illness didn't teach me my lesson. Over the Christmas holidays, I got foolishly drunk once again. In January, I spent three more weeks in hospital. Too fed up with school to do schoolwork, I read poetry, I wrote poetry, and I spent my less quiet hours listening to the burbling of an ancient madman in the next bed who had lost his mind to drink and venereal disease. It was then that I began reading *The Seven Storey Mountain* and saw in the life of a Catholic priest possibilities for myself that I'd not seen before.

It's easy for me to confuse what I found then with what I found in later readings, and those readings are overlaid by what Merton represented for me when I left the seminary at the end of five years and what he means to me now. But this is what I think I found at seventeen. At the same age, Thomas Merton's external life was very different from my own. His father came from New Zealand, his mother was from the United States. Both were artists, Protestant, and poor by choice. While they were studying in France with Percyval Tudor-Hart, Merton was born. His mother died when he was seven, and he grew up every which way, travelling with his father to Bermuda, living with his maternal grandparents and younger brother on Long Island, and living with his father in France before being sent away to a French boarding school and then to an English one. His father died when he was sixteen, leaving him with a guardian and a substantial allowance. He was very popular, witty, athletic, musically gifted, brilliant. My life was nothing like this. What we had in common beyond dead fathers and two shared initials — he was Thomas Feverel — was something I felt but could not express easily, something I was certain he would recognize in me if we ever met at the Monastery of Our Lady of Gethsemani, the place where he had gone to live the rest of his life as a cloistered monk after he'd done his own excessive drinking and just possibly fathered an illegitimate child. The bond between us seemed to me forged out of the battle we both waged against agonies of acute self-consciousness, of the search through reading and writing to ground our lives in something beyond the false and hypocritical, of the sense that within us there was another man who was always angry with the man we most wanted to be, of our judgement upon ourselves, that we transferred our wrath into overstatements we couldn't control, of the conviction that life was too precious and serious to be spent in false solemnity or play-acting. If our bond was this, more or less, it was also that neither of us was quite as ridden by Catholic guilt as others might be. For us, penance and denial weren't expiations so much as ways of building strength in the present for use in the future.

In the bleakest and blackest part of February 1962, when love seemed furthest out of reach, I decided I could do one of two things with the rest of my life: I could die of drink, despair, and general self-destruction in a couple of years, or I could become a Trappist monk, take vows of poverty, chastity, obedience, and silence, and put my big gift for words into books that would change the world and my smaller gift for love into learning how to work a potter's wheel. I liked the feel of wet clay spinning through my fingers. I'd never felt anything so sensuous in my life. I wanted to silence the sound of my polysyllabic voice. I went to see Father Walt to get the address of the Trappist Monastery of Our Lady of Gethsemani in Kentucky, in which Thomas Merton lived under vows of poverty, chastity, obedience, stability, and silence as the simple monk Father Louis. Father Walt sat me down, gave me a beer, lit my cigarette, and said he didn't think the Trappists would want me. The Trappists wanted young men who knew nothing of the world or older men who'd been to university. I didn't fit either category. And even if they wanted me, they couldn't take me without a reference letter from him, which he wasn't willing to write until I was older, smarter, wiser, a little more worldly and experienced. There were many who knocked on their door; few were let in. I'd stand a better chance if I had a bachelor's degree.

I hadn't thought of that. I'd just about given up the idea of going to university. University seemed beyond my financial reach. I didn't have the drive to do well at selling suits or anything else. I wasn't brilliant enough to win a major scholarship and lacked the muscles to work at the kind of summer labouring jobs that paid enough over the minimum wage to see me through the university year. I asked him what he thought about my going into the Franciscans instead; I'd heard they weren't as fussy about formal education.

Father Walt sized up my situation and made me a counter-offer. He didn't want me to settle for second best. He was now the rector of the cathedral. He'd pull some strings and get the archdiocese to help pay my way through university, but there were conditions attached. During the school year, I'd have to live in St. Pius X Seminary in Saskatoon with other young men who wanted to be parish priests. With them, I'd register for a BA at the University of Saskatchewan, take a major in philosophy through its affiliated St. Thomas More College, and seriously consider becoming a parish priest rather than a cloistered monk. During summer holidays, I'd have to earn as much money as I could and help out in the parish in my spare time. At the end of the three years, if I still wanted to become a monk, I'd be free to join Tom Merton in his monastery, with a decent BA and Father Walt's own letter of recommendation behind me.

I accepted a cup of coffee and shook his hand on a done deal, but not before we'd discussed the ramifications in detail. In asking me to consider becoming a parish priest, Father Walt appealed to my social conscience. He knew I had one. I had fairly solid credentials as a schoolboy orator and journalist. Debating nuclear disarmament on national radio with other high school students, I'd professed that I'd rather be Red than dead. The Medicare fight was raging in Saskatchewan, and I was on the far-left end of the CCF government's position, favouring civil service salaries rather than professional fees for doctors and fully socialized health care, British style. I had a pretty fair idea that Father Walt's views weren't far off mine. He wasn't saying much from his pulpit, given the deep divisions in our parish, but if push came to shove I knew he'd be one of the good guys. He was an Irish exile from Montreal. It was rumoured that in 1949, when he was a seminarian, he'd distributed leaflets on behalf of Archbishop Joseph Charbonneau urging the faithful to support the unionized workers in Asbestos, Quebec, in their strike against the Johns Manville Company and its strike-breaking tactics. Premier Maurice Duplessis championed the company against the workers, with the active endorsement of the majority of the clergy. When the Vatican removed Charbonneau and appointed Paul-Emile Léger to replace him, it was said that Father Walt found himself being encouraged to find employment in some other diocese, and that he'd chosen Regina because of Saskatchewan's CCF government. He had no political ambitions of his own, but he told me that if I did, I could still follow them as a priest. He added something I didn't know: under church law, a priest was relatively free to run for election to secular governing bodies. That was then; that was before Pope John Paul II had canon law altered to suit his own political agenda and barred priests from holding elected public office.

As I got up to leave, Father Walt posed some questions he had to ask pro forma for the letter he would write to the archbishop to put forth my candidacy for St. Pius X. I answered truthfully when he enquired about my personal morals but not quite as truthfully when he asked if I'd ever been a member of any subversive or heretical organizations. I'd been attending meetings of the Labour Progressive Party of Canada, *aka* the Communist Party, but I hadn't taken out a membership. I'd corresponded with the Ancient and Mystical Order Rosae Crucis. I said nothing of these or of the Baha'i information sessions and the Pentecostal prayer meetings I'd also attended. Entering the seminary was going to solve a lot of problems and end many confusions, I thought.

When I told what friends I had that I was going away to study to be a priest, some laughed, most shrugged, and Dido astonished me by breaking into tears. Dido was a good friend's girlfriend and Protestant, and her actual name is somewhat less classical. I had no idea why she was crying and was afraid of what she might say if I asked, so I didn't. I avoided her, beer, and most of my friends for the rest of the school year. On the night of my graduation dance, I took the transcontinental train to Ottawa. The Rotary Club was my sponsor for seven days of visits to parliament, meetings with cabinet ministers, banquets, and dances, with other students from across Canada. I'd placed second in a city-wide public speaking contest in which first prize was a trip to New York and the United Nations. Ottawa suited me just fine; I was fiercely anti-American. On the train home from Ottawa I met a cowgirl from Alberta who nearly changed my plans. She said she thought she could get her daddy to hire me on, and she'd teach me to ride. I still feel mild regret whenever I hear Ian Tyson sing "Summer Wages."

All through the summer, I played with clay a lot, practised saying less with simpler words, and spent empty hours listening to Gregorian chant when I wasn't dusting racks of unsold men's suits and helping out with the youth club, the altar boys, and other activities in the parish. In September, when I left for Saskatoon with my steamer trunk and a suitcase, Dido was on the same dayliner. She was going to study English and write poetry. Her boyfriend was staying behind in Regina. We talked. As the train pulled into the station, she kissed me and slipped a piece of pink paper in my pocket.

"My phone number. I'm living in residence."

"I don't think I'll be able to call you."

"Don't they let you date when you're in the seminary?"

"No."

"Call me anyhow. We can just talk."

TEN

403 Clarence Avenue North

St. Pius X Seminary was an old brick house at 403 Clarence Avenue North in Saskatoon, near the university. In the beginning, it had been a large and not particularly grand private home. Later, it had been an old folks' home. A fire escape attached to its side distinguished it from other houses on the street. Since 1957, it had housed men who wanted to be priests and two priests — the Rector and the Spiritual Director — who were supposed to show them the way. The first thing the Rector showed me was "The Rule of St. Pius X Seminary." The Rule was a set of mimeographed pages that laid down the regulations according to which we were to live in that house. The chief rule was that we had to strictly obey all the other rules unless there was a rule that required us not to obey it. In that case we were to obey the priests.

The Rule established order and discipline. It set a time to do everything; every day was timed to the minute. Each day was supposed to be the same as the previous one, and the last year of our three there was to be the same as the first.

AM

5:30   Wake-up / wash-up

6:00   Morning prayers / meditation

6:30   Mass / thanksgiving

7:15   Breakfast

7:45   End of Major Silence and recreation

8:15   Departure for classes

8:30   Classes or study

PM

12:00   Lunch

12:30   Recreation

1:00   Classes or study

4:30   Recreation

5:00   Rector's lecture

5:30   Prayer

6:00   Supper

6:30   Recreation

7:00   Study

9:00   Spiritual Director's lecture

9:45   Recreation

10:00   Start of Major Silence and bedtime

10:15   Lights out

A bell, actually a buzzer, would tell us when to start and when to stop each activity. It had to be answered immediately. This was the way we were to live, day after day after day, except Thursday afternoons, when studies were replaced by group athletics (always bruising, sometimes vicious: touch football, volleyball, basketball, or broomball, games of nine against nine) and Saturday afternoons, which we spent doing housework, attending choir practice, and confessing our sins after supper. On Sunday mornings, we were allowed an extra half-hour of sleep. Then, instead of study, we walked downtown to the cathedral, and our seminary choir practised a second time and sang the High Mass. On Sunday afternoons, the seminarians from Saskatoon were allowed visits from their families. The out-of-town guys could go out for a walk if we asked permission.

The Rule was equally specific about a lot of other things. White shirts, black ties, and black suits had to be worn outside the house at all times, unless we were on work or sports detail; cassocks — our basic black dresses — were to be worn everywhere inside the house except our bedrooms, the only place jeans were allowed. We weren't to speak, eat, listen to music, or have visitors in our bedrooms. We weren't allowed to make phone calls or receive them except in cases of emergency. The priests were entitled to open and read all incoming and outgoing mail. Recreation periods were to be spent in a group in the recreation area — a panelled basement with a hi-fi system, card tables, and overstuffed hand-me-down sofas and chairs in one room and a ping-pong table in another. We weren't to leave the house without the permission of one of the priests. We were to go everywhere in pairs and return as promptly as possible. We weren't to enter restaurants or to bring food into the seminary. What else? We weren't supposed to initiate any conversations with women and must terminate any conversation a woman started as swiftly and politely as possible. Such strictures went on for pages and pages.

The Rule seemed equally exhilarating and dismaying. I loved immediately and passionately everything that suggested the life of a solitary, silent, studious monk and hated on sight and no less passionately everything that forced me to hang around the other guys. As I read, Lawrence dragged his suitcases into the room. There were ten bedrooms for eighteen of us, two singles and eight doubles. Roommates were assigned, and Lawrence was to be mine. We'd met once at Father Walt's and hadn't hit it off. I didn't know who was on first or even to what league the Milwaukee Brewers belonged. He whistled "Take Me Out to the Ballgame" as he unpacked.

"We're supposed to be silent in our rooms."

"The Rule doesn't take effect until tonight. Hang loose."

"Fine. Let me put things bluntly, without finesse. There's nothing personal in this. I simply want to live like a monk. As far as I'm concerned, there's an invisible wall that runs through this room dividing it into two cells. Do you understand what I'm saying?"

"You want me to ignore you, is that it?"

"Forget I'm here."

"You don't have to be a prick about it."

I went back to studying the Rule. I'd never liked anybody at Campion who told me to hang loose. I'd always worn Jockeys, snug as possible.

Despite what I'd said, Lawrence figured he and I ought to be better friends. On the second Sunday he caught up with me after lunch and said he wanted to go for a walk.

"Where to?"

"I don't know. Anywhere. It doesn't really matter, does it?"

"I'd rather stay here and read a book."

"I already got permission for both of us."

Lawrence and I walked to the university. Conversation was halting. As we walked past the president's house to University Hospital, where the visitors' car park was overflowing, he said, "Geez, I wish I had a female visitor today, don't you?"

"No."

"I'd really like to see my mom and my sister. Who do you miss the most?"

"Nobody."

"That's not normal."

"I'm not interested in being normal."

"You aren't one of those kind, are you?"

"What kind?"

"You know, a guy who doesn't like women."

"I like women. I've had girlfriends. One of them is even in my Latin class."

"Sweet shit of Jesus, doesn't that give you problems? Don't you want to talk to her? I wish I knew some girl to talk to, even in Latin. I really miss women."

I did too, but I didn't say so. I had a hard time admitting to myself just how much I missed the conversation of women. Until my arrival in the seminary, I'd hardly ever spent a day in my life entirely apart from my mother or one or more of my six sisters. I'd never been away from my family before for more than the ten days I'd spent on my trip to Ottawa. I felt an emptiness where there had been a fullness. I tried to tell him about this.

Lawrence wanted to talk about the pain of sexual abstinence. His monologue took us from the hospital grounds to the Arts building to the library. At the library, I looked up the stairs longingly. I wanted to flee inside and immerse myself in books for the rest of the afternoon. A young woman in black tights and a blue duffle coat looked back over her shoulder as she opened the door. It was Dido. She smiled and waved and called my name. I waved and made a motion to suggest I was late for something and hurried on. Lawrence had to hurry to catch up with me.

"Who was that? Why didn't we stop and talk to her? Couldn't you see that she wanted to talk to us? Was that the girlfriend you mentioned?"

"Who?"

"That girl back there?"

"What girl? Did we see a girl?"

Lawrence wouldn't leave it alone. He wanted to know about Dido. Was she as pretty up close as she was from a distance? What was she built like above her nice legs? Had I ever made love to her, even a little — a French kiss, a good grope under her bra, a groin rub?

I confided nothing. We tramped on, me silent, Lawrence nattering about all the girls who'd left him aching, until we emerged at Varsity Stadium, crossed the road, and went into Wallings Restaurant and Variety. I was breaking a rule, but I needed to buy a carton of cigarettes. Lawrence would take two from the pack on my desk and leave a nickel. He kept saying he didn't smoke, not really, but I accumulated a lot of nickels. Lawrence spotted other seminarians who were breaking the rule against eating out, and he was sitting at their table by the time I'd bought my Peter Stuyvesants, a brand Lawrence seemed to like less than the more familiar Rothmans I'd been smoking. Joe had served in the Air Force. Phil had been a schoolteacher. Both were "delayed vocations," as new as we were to the seminary. They were eating cheeseburgers and french fries and drinking milkshakes. Lawrence ordered the same. I'd done my rule-breaking for the day and wanted to leave.

Some guys I'd drunk a few beers with in high school came in and ordered mid-afternoon fried egg and bacon breakfasts. The four of them shared a flat that still had room for me. They'd told me that when I'd told them I was going into the seminary. One of them was making book on my sticking it out till Christmas. While I looked over the odds, Lawrence left with Joe and Phil. I walked home alone.

That evening, after dinner, I was summoned to the Rector's office. The Rector said I'd been seen out walking on my own. He asked if I knew it was a very serious infringement against the Rule. I nodded. He asked if I realized that the punishment for breaking that rule was expulsion. I nodded. He asked if I wanted to be expelled. I hesitated. To this day I'm not sure why I didn't just nod my head again. A nod of the head, a hasty packing, a cab ride to my friends' flat, and I could have been seeing Dido that same night or drinking beer with better buddies than I figured I'd ever find inside the seminary. Or, even better, I could have hitched a ride to Alberta and found out exactly how good the weather was there in the fall, because if I'd left the seminary, I'd have had to earn some money somehow. But I didn't nod. I shook my head and was let off with a lecture on the dangers of being a loner and a warning that another infraction would bring automatic expulsion. I rushed to the nearest bathroom and puked my guts out. Ever since I'd stopped hurling abuse at people, I just threw up when I got really angry.

Keeping Lawrence invisible was easier than I'd expected. I always walked alongside someone else when we went back and forth to classes or the cathedral. When we played games, he was in the centre of the field, I was out near the sidelines. Whenever he got fidgety in our room, I opened Plato's *Republic* and slipped inside and away from him. Autumn turned to winter, we went home for Christmas, came back, and I immersed myself in my studies and kept doing all the things the Rule told us to do. When I went to bed at night, I was tired and I slept. It took more than a buzzer to wake me most mornings. Joe's room was next door, and he'd thump on the wall until he heard my feet hit the floor. He was a light sleeper.

Very early one February morning, I was suddenly, horribly wide awake. Lawrence was bending over my bed, his hands tight around my throat, his thumbs pressing down against my windpipe, strangling me. I couldn't scream, could hardly breathe. He was too strong to shake off, so I kicked out and connected with my bookcase. The tumble of textbooks woke Joe. He flung open our door, switched on the lights, grabbed Lawrence in a hammerlock, and broke the stranglehold.

"Let me kill him. I have to kill him, he never shuts up. He talks all night. Make him shut up! He's evil!"

Joe, Lawrence, and I had been joined by a dozen others, including the Rector. We stopped to listen. The only thing any of us could hear was the wind off the river rattling the ill-fitting window in our room.

Once Lawrence was sedated, safely out of the house, and in a hospital bed, the Rector called me to his office. I was still shaking. He didn't seem to notice. He just said, "Don't worry about what happened tonight. Lawrence was sick. You don't have to tell anybody anything else."

"What else is there to say?"

"That's the spirit!"

"I'm sorry, I'm not getting something. Is there something I'm supposed to know?"

"Lawrence felt very guilty about trying to get you expelled at the beginning of the year."

"He didn't do much. He should have waited for me so I didn't have to walk home alone, that's all."

"You really don't know?"

"Know what?"

"Lawrence was the one who reported that you'd gone for a walk on your own."

"Why would he do that?"

"He had a mental illness. He was probably afraid you'd find out."

"Why didn't you tell me? He could have killed me."

"We're all in the hands of God. We're the clay. We're only His clay."

That's probably not quite what he said. That's more likely an expression of my tendency to embroider a story with more symmetry than the real world usually delivers. Remembering the Rector's penchant for never missing an opportunity to impress upon us the sufferings that had to be endured in serving God, it's more likely that he spoke to me of the crosses we have to bear for Christ's sake. He probably said something like this: "You must have greater faith in our Saviour. He sent you this cross to test the strength of your vocation. Always remember, our blessed Saviour was tested fourteen times along the route to His crucifixion. You must be prepared for the same. Go in peace. You've passed your first station on the way of the cross He has laid out for you."

The Rector was almost Buddha-like in his capacity for seeing the world as suffering. But Buddha-like he wasn't when it came to compassion. He didn't look at the discolorations developing on my neck, he didn't look at the deeper bruises in my eyes. He didn't say anything comforting. He told me to get back to bed. Although Lawrence and Joe and Phil and some others called him Tex or Father Bob, I always called him Father Ogle, except on one occasion when my lips spoke my mind and I called him Father Ogre to his face. He winced. But an ogre he was, and not just to me, throughout my two of the seven years he served as Rector of St. Pius X Seminary. He said as much in his autobiography *North/South Calling:* "Though I think I treated them in a strange, over-powering way, I like to think that they saw through the Rule, into the real quality that makes up the essence of human friendship." No, I didn't. He passes over his years at the seminary in a page, and only one of the fifty-nine black and white photographs show him with a group of seminarians, me included. In 1979, when I last saw him, fifteen years after he'd left the seminary to go to Brazil, encountered him for the first and only time on an equal footing and called him "Bob" even though he'd been elected NDP member of parliament for Saskatoon East just three days earlier, we had more to say to one another over breakfast than we'd found to talk about in the two years we'd lived under the same roof. He said I'd changed a lot, but it was obvious to both of us that he'd changed much more. I've never known another man who altered so much through his middle years, grew so much more percep-tive, gained so enormously in compassion. But as Rector, he was very strange, very overbearing, inflexible to a fault, incapable of negotiating much of anything, very priestly. He died of a cancer that put him to a great deal of suffering before it killed him. We exchanged letters after *A Blue Boy in a Black Dress* was published and he'd become ill. We said goodbye in a spirit of something very like friendship.

During most of our first year together at St. Pius X, the Rector made an example of me in his daily lectures to such an extent that I kept missing the generality of the point he was using me to exemplify. The point was his total commitment to the cult of the priest as holy warrior. These days, the word cult has almost entirely lost the meaning it once had for Catholics: a devotion or homage to a person or thing possessing a special relationship to Jesus — the cult of Mary, the cult of the Sacred Heart. The Rector never imagined being anything other than a priest, and he knew only one way of being one, the way he'd learned in his seven years at St. Peter's Seminary, London, Ontario, from 1946 to 1953: a way that was Army-like, soldierly, militant, militaristic. When the Rector talked about being a priest, he spoke always of being in the trenches, being on the firing line, going into battle, being shot down in flames. When he spoke of the dangers a priest faced, he spoke of whisky as a bomb and emotional attachments as depth charges that could blow a priest out of the water. To survive these and all other perils, a priest could not stand alone. He had to be part of a squad, stick with the troop, follow orders, trust the Commander-in-Chief. It was the language of the returned soldiers with whom he'd been a seminarian and of the soldier priests with whom he'd mingled while writing his thesis, *Faculties of Canadian Military Chaplains,* for a doctorate in Canon Law. It wasn't the happy Irish sentimentality that Hollywood hit paydirt with whenever Pat O'Brien, Spencer Tracey, or Bing Crosby were cast as priests. The Rector was Big John Wayne leading the troops at the Battle of the Bulge. And I fell into line. I learned that the herd's initial sympathy for a victim soon gives way to the suspicion that the victim had it coming to him, had done something too provocative, too independent, too eccentric. I tried to fall into line.

Looking back, I wonder what kept me going through the motions. It certainly wasn't that the seminary had great or even pleasant facilities. The rooms were dull, utilitarian, little altered since they'd done nursing home duty, scarcely distinguishable from one another. All had brown-painted metal bedsteads. The bed coverings were cheap, coarse, heavy-duty Army blankets. Beside each bed was a school desk on which a bookshelf was mounted, a straight-backed oak chair, a chest of drawers, a small mirror. Towel rails hung from the closet doors. Walls were painted the same shade of green in every room, and all the floors were covered with the same mottled green linoleum. Eighteen of us shared three bathrooms. The bathrooms had single washbasins, toilets, and bathtubs with shower heads. By washing at either at the basin or the tub, we each got four or five minutes between five-thirty and six every morning. The parlour, porch, and front entrance were normally out of bounds, reserved for the priests and visitors. We came and went through a door at the back, which connected the basement to the yard. This was our entrance and exit at all seasons of the year, except for that day, if it came, when one of us left permanently. In the days before the whole world knew about Timothy Leary, it was called "dropping out," and the last exit was always through the front door. After that you were "lost" — as dead to the rest of the squad as if you'd fallen in battle.

It was a big house and a draughty one, heated by an archaic forced-air heating system which blew great clouds of warm dust from one room to another. In the depths of a Saskatoon winter, I'd go to bed dressed in tennis socks, a suit of thermal underwear, a full-length flannel nightgown, and frequently a woollen watch cap. Even so, I sometimes woke up with the numb white ears and nose of incipient frostbite.

We couldn't make it warmer, but we were supposed to keep it clean. I tried. I did try to learn to do housework, but I was quite hopeless. At home, I'd never done more than make my bed. My chores had always been down in the basement or out in the yard. But in the seminary, we did all the housework outside the kitchen. Every room was cleaned and polished every Saturday, starting with our bedrooms. Our private space had to pass an army-style inspection by the Rector, who tackled his obligation with the zest of a drill sergeant. If a bedroom failed to measure up, if the coin failed to bounce on the bedding, the finger to stay clean as it ran along the surfaces, the occupant must scrape the previous week's wax from the tiled hallways with table knives and razor blades. This is not made up. Table knives. Razor blades. Once the wax had been removed, the floor was washed and waxed again, then polished. If your room passed inspection, you got to clean a bathroom, the dining room, the parlour, the chapel, in ascending order of housekeeping skills. The fortunate few who excelled at housework went to neighbouring convents and parish offices to do special chores and were rewarded with music on the radio, roast beef sandwiches, beer, chocolates, a look at the Saturday newspaper, sometimes a television show. I experienced none of it. My room never passed inspection that first year. At home for the summer, I came into the kitchen wearing a knee-length housecoat. My mother looked at my knees and could not believe her eyes. From all the praying and all the scraping, I had the worst case of housemaid's knee she'd ever seen. She wept and insisted that I show my legs to Father Walt.

ELEVEN

1963 and Dr. B.

If 1963 marks the true beginning of that peculiarly engorged era of intercourse now called "the Sixties," I really didn't notice it. It wasn't that the Sexual Revolution, with its conspicuous consumption of sticky joys and smelly comforts, was slower coming to Regina than elsewhere, or that I wasn't noticing women. Home from the seminary for the summer, I learned that Men's Clothing no longer required my services at Simpson's, and I was transferred to Women's and Children's Shoes. It was a very unerotic job. While buying shoes, women are too self-absorbed and annoying to be sultry and seductive, and squalling children with leaking diapers are definitely the downside of baby-making. Outside working hours, I focused my attention on other forbidden fruits we didn't get in the seminary: news of the world, unrestricted reading, interesting music.

Before Vatican II (which began its first session on October 11, 1962, just a few weeks after I'd entered Saint Pius X), Catholics were incessantly and severely taught that there was no salvation outside the church. Under Pope Pius XII, the emphasis had always fallen on enhancing the power of the church in the world by divine right. Pius XII was first, last, always God's own Emperor. That meant among other things that no book could be published for Catholic readers unless Vatican-certified censors had examined it to ensure that it didn't go against faith or morals or cause scandal. Authors who published without subjecting their work to official censorship risked having their work placed on the Index of Prohibited Books and themselves excommunicated.

Excommunication was and remains the most extreme punishment of the Roman Church — exile from earthly communion and heavenly reward. Catholic books had to carry two written permissions — *Nihil obstat* (nothing impedes) and *Imprimatur* (let it be published) — granted by church authorities in the place of publication. In the United States, therefore, a lot of Catholic publications originated outside New York, away from the direct influence of Francis Joseph Cardinal Spellman, who liked to think of himself as the J. Edgar Hoover of the religious domain. Because the spiritual and material interpenetrate, Spellman and Hoover were very good friends and allies in many causes. Catholic publishers did not lean very far to the left except in the boondocks — Collegeville, Minnesota, or Gethsemani, Kentucky.

The church informed its members what movies they could see without sin through Legion of Decency ratings that appeared weekly in Catholic newspapers. Live and recorded performances were much more difficult to regulate. Cardinal Spellman was one of Lenny Bruce's favourite targets; Spelly's alleged penchant for rough trade in male prostitutes provided Bruce with lots of juicy barbs at risky episcopal behaviour. Could a devout Catholic listen to Bruce's albums without sin? Could a devout Catholic listen without sin to Tom Lehrer's satirical "Vatican Rag" and laugh at "Drink the wine and chew the wafer / Two, four, six, eight / Time to transubstantiate"? Catholics were generally advised to follow the dictates of their parish priest and, failing that, their own consciences. In the seminary, little was left to our consciences. Permission to read any book not included on a university syllabus had to be obtained from the Spiritual Director, who was liberal but not very literary beyond his knowledge of Kafka. Novels not included in the English reading lists came under the dominion of the Rector. Permission to listen to music was also in the hands of the Rector, who controlled access to television, radio, newspapers, and magazines, all of which were simply forbidden to us unless he felt our lives might be enhanced by something especially important, such as the Stanley Cup finals or the Grey Cup game or, remarkably, the first appearance of the Beatles on *Ed Sullivan.*

The Rector had provided a stereo hi-fi system for the recreation room but objected to most forms of popular music. If records were by women, they gave rise to lust. If they were by black performers, they were crude or raucous or mournful when they weren't plainly and simply morbid. Blues — the devil's music. Modern jazz — satanic. So he'd heard and fervently believed. I donated a small collection of Kingston Trio and other folkie records to the seminary to get some small relief from the Norman Luboff choir, Mitch Miller, and the gunfighter ballads of Tex Ritter, Marty Robbins, and Jim Reeves that the Rector really enjoyed. So "Tom Dooley" and "Puff the Magic Dragon" got added to a play list that included a stack of albums by the Weavers that somebody else had donated. As anyone who has ventured into any youth-oriented Catholic church service in the last thirty-five years can attest, similar sounds must have taken hold of the ears of seminarians and priests and nuns from one end of the continent to another, more or less simultaneously. They gave rise to a genre of strummed church music that veers sharply from the annoying to the truly weird. One of the less folkish and more pop-minded of the seminarians in Ottawa set his Folk Mass partially to the tune of "House of the Rising Sun," a song on Bob Dylan's first album. Dylan got it from Dave Van Ronk, who had gotten it from a Mississippi blues singer. The song was about a brothel seen from a woman's point of view until Eric Burdon of the Animals brutally turned it into a catamite's howl that hit #1 on the Billboard charts in 1965, a year before it got turned into a "Credo."

The two news stories that I was interested in researching at the Regina Public Library in the summer of 1963 were the defeat of John Diefenbaker's Conservative government in the April general election and the sidetracking of the curia's agenda at Vatican II. Both had connections to the nuclear arms race. The central issue of the Canadian federal election was the equipping of our troops with American nuclear weapons at home and abroad. Diefenbaker's government foresaw Canada serving only as a peacekeeper. Lester Pearson defeated the Conservatives with help from the Kennedy White House and thereby compromised our sovereignty. Diefenbaker was easy to dislike, but those opposed to nuclear proliferation admired his government's defence of Canadian sovereignty.

Vatican II was less of a disappointment. Only the third since the Reformation, it was far and away the most global. Given that it aimed to bring together about twenty-four hundred bishops and another hundred general superiors of religious orders, it seemed likely to be unwieldy and doomed before it even met. Every priest I knew thought the council was simply going to rubber stamp long-anticipated changes in regulations regarding the substitution of the vernacular for Latin in church services and seminary education and clear up some longstanding problems in the church's law code. The first session of the council opened in a hostile atmosphere influenced by the Cuban missile crisis: strong pressures to address the morality of nuclear war firmly faced equally strong pressures from Cardinal Spellman and his allies to say nothing that would compromise American military supremacy. The man in the middle was Pope John XXIII.

These days, John XXIII is said to have opened the windows of the church. That's sort of like saying Bob Dylan wrote "Blowing in the Wind" without mentioning that his song became an anthem of the Civil Rights movement. John XXIII tried to air the place out, to expel the lingering stench of fascism and militarism from a Eurocentric church. That was his agenda. The first session of Vatican II is sandwiched between his two great encyclicals: the call for social justice in 1961 in *Mater et Magistra,* and the plea for peace in *Pacem in terris* on April 10, 1963. These papal teachings absolutely oppose nuclear weapons and racism. It wasn't just the Cuban missile crisis that influenced the council: Adolf Eichmann, the mastermind behind moving the Jewish people out of their homes into the ghettoes and then into the concentration camps, was on trial in Jerusalem, and Hannah Arendt's articles made it plain that, while Nazism had driven the world mad, its perpetrators remained perfectly sane and logical to a fault. Before the Council even met, John XXIII remedied one specific kind of racism in the church by ordering the deletion of all anti-Jewish references from the liturgy.

I sometimes wonder if Steven Spielberg's interest in "righteous gentiles" might lead him one day to cast Bob Hoskins as Joseph Roncalli, aka Pope John XXIII, and make a movie about Roncalli's efforts to save Jews in Istanbul during the war and his later attempt to extirpate religious intolerance and racial hatred of Jews from the Vatican and the church. As Pope, John XXIII used his considerable influence to persuade Catholics that the plight of Jews after the war was truly without precedent in human history: Jews as a people were victims not only of genocide but also of unparalleled spiritual degradation. To be a Jew under the Nazis was to be ridiculed by the press, insulted by the populace, defamed by religious authorities, prosecuted by the judiciary for a fact of birth and not a personal action, ritually humiliated by the police, brutalized by the military, starved and slaughtered by the penal authorities. To be a Jew under the Nazis was to have the full power of society and civil and military law turned against you. While I was reading back issues of *The New Yorker* and other magazines to find out what exactly had happened at the Council, John XXIII died. On June 3, his influence fading with his breath, the statement on the Jewish people he'd personally had Cardinal Bea draft for the Council encountered stiff opposition. Eventually it was passed in a version so watered down that some Catholics, especially Polish Catholics and their leaders, regard Auschwitz as an especially grievous instance of human brutality and not as an unprecedented devastation of the spiritual order supposed to prevail in even a nominally Christian culture.

Nobody knew what was likely to happen under Paul VI, another imperial prince of the Pius XII model, who was crowned on June 30, 1963. The world was moving in so many different directions — and the church with it — that the Rector figured the seminarians in his charge should be better informed. Over the summer, he started subscriptions to a number of magazines. When I returned in the fall, I was put in charge of them and the rest of the seminary library and absolved of all housework except keeping my own room straight. Even then, my bed never got more than a cursory glance. I suspected that the Rector had been warned. Premature arthritic damage to my knees had been diagnosed by the doctor I was sent to see after Father Walt had examined my knees.

When the seminary lights went out at night, the Rector's shadow retreated, only to be replaced by others. Lawrence, my attacker, was gone, but his memory lingered. We'd spoken over the summer. He hadn't apologized for trying to strangle me. In fact, he'd accused me of causing his breakdown by being too quiet, an impossible roommate. He said he could never tell what I was thinking. The Rector seemed to agree. I was assigned one of the two single bedrooms, the closest accommodation that the big house had to monastery cells.

In my pokey room in a gable under the eaves at the back of the house, the ceiling sloped so low over the bed that I couldn't sit up without bumping my head. The branches of the large tree outside its small window touched the glass in a strong wind. On the other side of the tree, almost at eye level, a street lamp reflected off the mirror every time the curtains moved with the wind that seeped in through the gable's many cracks and crevices. It was more box than bedroom, but I was happy to have its privacy. Talking things over with Lawrence hadn't freed me of the nightmares his attack precipitated. And he'd left another legacy. While packing his belongings, I'd found some small brown medicine bottles. Most were empty, all were carefully hidden in the folds of shirts and the insides of socks and shoes. When I found a full bottle, I popped a couple of pills to test their effect. Bliss. Tranquility. I got my own prescription from the University Health Clinic.

The pills, garden-variety tranquillizers, didn't take the nightmares away, but they made it easier to get back to sleep after I felt Lawrence's hands around my neck again and began to sweat. They also seemed to lower my body temperature. The chill in the air got to me earlier that autumn than ever before. When the winds from the north really began to blow, I was colder than I'd ever been elsewhere in that draughty old house. A couple of extra blankets didn't help. Waking from nightmares, I'd be wet, but the bed felt like a lump of ice. Sometimes I wouldn't even bother going back to bed. I'd sit up and write by the light of the street lamp. A new album, *Freewheelin' Bob Dylan*, had considerable impact. Dylan seemed to move effortlessly from the public to the private. He could write of the hard rain coming and his girl of the north country, and the political didn't conflict with the personal. My own poetry and crude attempts at song lyrics moved every which way except to the heart. Strident or soppy, they were neurotic, obsessive, fixated on Dido and her breasts as missiles aimed right at my fidelity. All that summer I'd avoided going anywhere I might see her.

Then one night when my eyes opened on my nightmare, I thought I could see Dido's face, shining, blurred, indistinct, but stiff, blue with death. She hovered above me, and I saw she wasn't Dido but somebody who was dead. In the morning I told myself I'd imagined her, but she was there in the same place the next night. The night after that I wore my glasses to sleep. I wanted to see my vision clearly until I actually opened my eyes and looked right into the face of a woman who was definitely not alive, a glacial face shining with a silver light. I fled my bed, trailing my bathrobe behind me down three flights of stairs. In the recreation room, one of the third-year seminarians was reading Descartes's *Meditations* and blowing smoke rings.

"What's wrong?"

"I had a really bad dream. Somebody was in my room with me, trying to get into my bed. When I opened my eyes, I saw a ghost."

"You did."

"I just said I did."

"I mean I know you did. That was my room last year. An old lady died in that bed. If you say the rosary, she'll pray along with you."

"Are you kidding?"

"If you don't want her hanging around, sprinkle holy water on the blankets every night, that's all you have to do. It'll keep her away."

"Are you kidding?"

"Ask Tex if you don't believe me."

"He knows about it?"

"He knows everything in this place. He knows we're talking right now."

"How would he know that?"

"I'm always down here. He saw you go by his door."

"What are you doing here?"

"I can't sleep at night. I study."

"And the Rector lets you?"

"Sure. I don't know why you have so many problems with him. But what about this? Do you understand Descartes?"

I explained as well as I could why the Cartesian soul makes contact with the Cartesian body in the pineal gland.

There was only one warm room in the entire seminary, and luckily its light was on when I went back upstairs. This was the room occupied by the older of the two priests who lived with us. He held the title of Spiritual Director and was in charge of our religious well-being. I called him Doctor B. He liked that. It reminded him of Kafka. He had nicknames for all of us. He called me Fritz. Dr. B. was at prayer. I stepped inside and asked him to hear my confession. I told him I'd just broken the Major Silence. He said I should see him in the morning. When I did, we had a long discussion about ghosts and a longer one about Jungian archetypes, especially the *anima.*

Dr. B. was Hungarian by birth and served in the German army as a boy soldier in the final months of the war. As the invading Allies pushed north from Sicily, he'd made his way to Rome as a deserter and entered a Vatican house of study, where he excelled in theology, earning a doctorate. After the Hungarian Revolution, he'd found refuge in Canada as a theological adviser to the bishop of Saskatoon. He found Saskatchewan very cold. His room was a fortress against the winds raging elsewhere in that house. His floor was carpeted wall-to-wall with broadloom. His window was fitted with heavy drapes. His own chair and the two for visitors were equipped with knitted lap rugs. Twin portable electric heaters supplemented the radiator. They provided real heat and some of the feel of an open fire. Although Dr. B. professed total ignorance and incompetence in all things technical, mechanical, and domestic, he heightened intimacy through the skilled use of indirect lighting. Snugly dressed in a heavy black cardigan, a black shirt with clerical collar attached, and neatly pressed black wool trousers, his feet encased in sheepskin bedroom slippers, he'd sit and read for hours on end from the hundreds of theological treatises that lined his walls, making voluminous notes.

Dr. B. was passionate about theology. He loved it in all its branches. Versed in the classical traditions of Augustine and Thomas Aquinas, he found his real interest in the avant garde theologians who dominated the post-war period: Bonhoeffer, Barth, Tillich, but most of all Karl Rahner and the new generation of theologians and biblical scholars who'd been thrust into the limelight by Vatican II. Among them was Hans Küng. Dr. B. was especially fond of Küng, not least because they'd been seminarians together. Küng had actually served at Dr. B.'s first Mass.

It must have bothered him a great deal more than he ever intimated to us that he was so far from Rome at that moment in history. He was one of an international brotherhood of theologians who had been effectively ignored by the Vatican prior to the council. Since he could not be present alongside the others in Rome, he kept in touch through a stream of correspondence. He spent his days at his desk, keeping abreast of the second session of debates, which had started on September 29, 1963. In the evenings, he was available to us. At his desk, his door open, his Grundig radio tuned to the evening concert on the CBC, he'd sit absorbed by the treatise in front of him until one of us came to visit. We were obliged to have a private conference with him once a month. A few of us tried to see him more often. Whenever I arrived, he would welcome me profusely, see me settled, take up his book again — usually Karl Rahner — and read aloud until he'd completed whatever disputed question he was studying. Then he'd translate what he'd read from the German, paraphrase the passage, condense the arguments, place the issue in historical context, and question me on it. We'd begin to chat, and I'd lay my inner life bare. Then he'd speak to me formally, but now with warmth that first rivalled, then surpassed the temperature of his room. Haltingly, as he translated his thoughts from his native Magyar into English, his voice would gather strength and firmness, confident in its effect. And the effect was always dramatic. Dr. B. had a wonderful capacity to relate personal anxieties to the larger problems of mankind, making his hearer feel less distant from the general fate of modern man. I soon developed a crush, something that had never happened to me as a schoolboy among Jesuits.

There was nothing overtly erotic about our relationship. I tried to model my mind on Dr. B.'s mind and read what he read, argue as he argued. To keep himself healthy and to add what European flavour he could to seminary meals, Dr. B. carried cloves of garlic with him and sliced them into the food — his own portion and the portions of whomever he thought lacked inner fire. He also sprinkled paprika liberally wherever he thought it was needed. To those who objected, he'd pose the following argument:

> A theologian must have a healthy mind, and a healthy mind needs a healthy body. Raw garlic keeps the body healthy. Ergo, theologians must eat raw garlic. If you refuse to eat raw garlic, your body will grow weak and your mind will go out of balance, and your theology will become as dangerous to your health as a Saskatoon winter.

If you could create an equally strong counter-argument, he left your food alone. I didn't even try. I shared some of his tastes in food and all of his appetite for abstract knowledge, including psychology. I felt a great need to understand what had happened to Lawrence, what it was to be diagnosed manic-depressive or paranoid or lumbered with any of the other labels psychiatry attached to the maladapted and dysfunctional.

When I had a study period between university classes, I'd duck into the Reserve Reading Room and work my way through readings attached to psychology courses. This was the year of my great intellectual awakening. My second-year courses in biological sciences, logic, ethics, Virgil's *Georgics* in Latin, and a survey of modern philosophy from Montaigne to Kant weren't enough. In the fifteen minutes between classes and whenever I was on the toilet, I was also reading *Tristram Shandy*. In my first year, I'd interpreted the rule about talking to women too liberally. I'd been willing to tutor anyone in any of my classes but made myself too available to female philosophy students.

The Rector ordered me to stop talking to varsity women unless I absolutely could not avoid it. So I read and read and read. And whenever I could snatch some minutes away from card games during recreation, I worked at improving the seminary library.

It really needed a good sorting out. The books had been donated, many from the estates of dead priests whose intellects had not been too lively. Shelves were chock-a-block with out-of-date treatises, textbooks, works of devotion and spirituality, bestselling novels, and practical guides to everything a priest might be called upon to do, from writing a sermon to building a church to dining in high society. Boxes and boxes of books in the basement hadn't yet been sorted. With Dr. B.'s guidance, I winnowed the shelves and unpacked everything in storage and gleefully burned anything damaged or out-of-date. I literally threw them in an incinerator in the backyard and watched them burn by the box load. Most were so old and dried out that the splendid flames tended more to blue than yellow or pink. In those days, Saskatoon was a city full of backyard incinerators. Even so, neighbours were curious to know what the young man in the black dress was so maniacally burning most mornings. Some jumped to the conclusion that this was church censorship at work and said as much. One of the reproachful ones was William Hoffer, who lived a couple of houses over and who later went on to be a knowledgeable collector and dealer in Canadian books. Professor Abram Hoffer, William's father, came to the seminary as a guest speaker to outline his clinical research into alcoholism and schizophrenia and his LSD and megavitamin therapies. I listened attentively, studied the bibliography he provided, and learned too much about LSD ever to be enthusiastic about dropping acid, even after I eventually dropped out of the seminary.

I was going to drop out three years sooner than I did. I really thought I was going to leave by the front door before the end of that second year. I'd had enough of living under those conditions. Not speaking to women meant that the ghost gave way to Dido parading undressed through my dreams, joined by more and more of my female classmates, all equipped now with the bodies of *Playboy* centrefolds summoned up from pre-seminary wankings. I felt myself losing control. I counted down the days until the last of the final exams and imagined the beautiful bonfire I would make with my black dresses and my undertaker's suits, and I wrote a farewell letter I was going to leave behind for the Rector.

A few days short of the day I intended to declare closing time on my sojourn as a priest-in-training, all of us were summoned to a special meeting with the Rector, who announced his departure for Brazil as part of a missionary team. I sent my cassocks and suits to the dry cleaners, but I did use the incinerator to purify myself. I threw into the flames all the pictures and cartoons, diaries and journals, poems and stories I'd drawn and written in the seminary and most of what I'd composed during my high-school years. They seemed to me ugly and dishonest, worthless. I'd just finished rereading *The Seven Storey Mountain,* paying special attention to the passage where Merton sets fire to his own past in the furnace of the college where he taught before entering the Abbey of Gethsemani.

The principal reason why I decided to stay on was that I suspected I could be good at living a priest's life, far better than I'd been able to prove to the Rector, with his kneejerk reverence for obedience, or prove to myself, with my propensity for wet dreams inspired by fantasies of a parade of naked women winding back upon itself in a labyrinth out of an Escher etching. I wanted to become contemplative. I wanted to experience the power that drew Thomas Merton to convert to the Catholic Church, the truth he unearthed by studying its wisest writers, the beauty he found in its prayers, the goodness he found in living a communal life. I thought I could experience a holiness that didn't crush my ego or disembody my mind. I thought I could begin to be of some real use to others.

TWELVE

Undoubtedly Thomist

Nobody knows where roads not taken might have led, but when I consider what could have happened had I left the seminary at the end of my second year, I suspect I might have moved in with those friends who had the flat with room for me and completed my BA in philosophy, gone on to law school, and articled in Regina with a firm whose senior partner I'd come to know through volunteer work in my home parish. My grades and oratorical skills had impressed him, and he'd not so subtly let me know that he and his colleagues would shoulder the costs of my further education in return for joining their firm on graduation. It was an excellent offer, and I'm still flattered that he made it. As a lawyer, I hope I would have involved myself with the New Democratic Party and worked on the leading edge of social reform. That's to say, I like to think I wouldn't have taken a less noble road as a lawyer and human being, that I wouldn't have squandered my talents to further the partisan interests of the mainline parties while feathering a very cosy nest for myself in a Lakeview mansion. That's also to say that I trust I wouldn't have gotten one of my classmates pregnant, married too young, and ended up as an embittered school administrator or social worker, hating my job, my wife, and my diminished life, and over-indulging grandchildren as compensation.

If I'd followed any of these roads or country lanes, or even dived into the deep end of pork-barrel politics, it's likely that I'd have remained in contact with some of the others who lived at Saint Pius X when I was there: Saskatchewan is a kind of province-wide village for those of my generation who didn't move to Calgary. And when we got together at barbecues, I suspect we'd reminisce easily about those years we'd shared under Tex's regimen. Talk could turn on things like food — the groaning tables of soup, roast turkey, lamb, baked fish, ham, mashed potatoes, all the fixings, and special desserts the nuns in the kitchen prepared lovingly for their boys. What we'd recollect most vividly would be the bread and the Spam. The nuns baked bread for us three times a week, loaves and loaves of it. The bread that didn't get eaten between bakings got used up as stuffing in roast fish on Fridays and roast turkey on Sundays or made over with milk and raisins and cinnamon apples in bread puddings. I liked those bread puddings far better than any of the other desserts. None of us had ever eaten so much fresh bread in our lives. Or fish. Or turkey. Or Spam. The Spam was actually Diefenbacon, our name for the government surplus preserved pork that the Diefenbaker government had distributed to charitable institutions to lessen a mountain of the stuff that had accumulated through some Liberal government excess at honest-to-goodness pig troughs. There were cases and cases of this mock ham at the seminary, more than our fair allotment, because whenever the inmates of another Catholic institution — usually a convent — had rebelled and wouldn't eat any more of it, they dumped it on the seminary. Spam and eggs. Spam and beans. Spam fried rice. Egg foo Spam. Spam and Spam. I suspect we'd also swap tales of Dr. B. that few of our wives, lovers, or children would altogether comprehend without having felt firsthand the intellectual heat and passion he brought to our lives.

Though we might spend late-night hours discussing the church and why I stopped or why they continued attending services, I never imagine myself saying anything not superficial or trivial about my experience, anything going much beyond its strange militarism and my personal conflicts with the Rector. I needed three more years in the seminary to get to the heart of my life and many more to begin to understand and unravel what I found there, even though these years led me into the shadow of death, leaning out over the dark waters of the Ottawa River.

In September 1964, I started my final year at Pius X. The Rector's replacement was a newly ordained priest, a member of the first class to graduate from Pius X. Father Jim introduced changes in the daily life of the place that were subtle and sweet, especially in our prayer life. For him, becoming a Catholic priest didn't demand the regimentation so necessary for Father Ogle. Father Jim made the chapel a finer place to worship and pray. Adopting the changes permitted by the decree on liturgy at Vatican II, he renovated the altar, bought new vestments, made changes in the order of service, and introduced chanting as an alternative to private devotional exercises. The claims made for Transcendental Meditation as a method of stress reduction and memory enhancement probably can be doubled for liturgical chant.

I don't know what happens if you just listen to it. I don't know if people who made *Canto Gregoriano* an international bestseller in the 1990s heard it as anything other than a more tuneful, less aimless, more joyful, less pointless, more shapely white noise than the general run of New Age aural wallpaper. Chant brings a blessing to the singer, but it's debatable how much blessing it sprinkles on listeners. Group chanting is very hard work. It demands a degree of excellence — no mistakes — that it then takes for granted. Natural talent is far less important than mental focus, and less able voices are at par with better ones, because the objective of chant is to create a collective voice with nothing extraneous in it. It isn't harmonic; the sounds remain distinct.

It's minimalist, sure, but chanting is the closest I've ever come to making music in my bones. Monks who have devoted their lives to it claim that the resonance Gregorian chant sets up in the bones of the chanter pacifies the body and focuses the mind. This effect was a rudder for the development of chant and is as separable from textual or symbolic significance as it is indifferent to religious orientation. There's evidence that chanting can be used to correct perceptual and attention disorders. When I was eleven, I was in a boys' Gregorian choir under the direction of a Franciscan friar. During those eighteen months, I made remarkable progress as a student, gaining concentration, confidence, and speed. The chanting Father Jim introduced into the daily life of the seminary was a simplification of the kind long practised in monasteries: in English, we chanted some of the sacred hours of the monastic day — lauds before breakfast, sext at noon, vespers before supper, compline before bed. I've never been happier in my studies nor more successful.

The downgrading of Latin as the language of worship and priestly instruction by Vatican II meant that I didn't have to continue studying it. In its place, I took psychology. I was also taking courses in economics, metaphysics, the history of philosophy in the middle ages, and the philosophy of nature. The economist was a Canadian nationalist and socialist; the psychologist had an existentialist streak; the metaphysician was slightly mad, thoroughly eccentric, enormously witty and insightful, a man who studied Marshall McLuhan as assiduously as he pondered Plato; the medieval historian laid on a daunting workload; and the lectures in the philosophy of nature were close readings of Alfred North Whitehead by a mathematician and logician. All five professors were priests, members of the Congregation of Saint Basil — the religious order that founded St. Michael's College in Toronto in 1852. The

Basilians are one of the lesser publicized glories of the Catholic Church in Canada. The Congregation of St. Basil arose out of a secret school in the mountains of central France, near the city of Annonay, that opened in 1822 and operated in defiance of the French Revolution. Bishop de Charbonnel of Toronto, who had been a student at the Annonay school, invited his former confrères to Toronto to open St. Michael's and offer, in the French style, a combination of high school and university education. The Basilians made St. Michael's the leading English-speaking Catholic institution of higher learning in what was to become Canada. Then they extended their educational range and influence by taking control of Assumption College in Windsor in 1870 and establishing St. Thomas More as a federated college of the University of Saskatchewan, in Saskatoon, in 1936. At the same time, the order served parishes in Hamilton, London, Sault Ste. Marie, Calgary, Edmonton, Nelson, and Vancouver; in several dioceses in the United States; and in a Latin American apostolate in the USA, Mexico, and Columbia. Today, St. Thomas More College claims that it explores the "riches of revelation and of nature so that the united endeavour of intelligence and faith will enable people to come to the full measure of their humanity." It also asserts its dedication to synthesizing "faith and reason in all aspects of the human condition" in an "inclusive community." The Basilians' educational goals and their humility of expression haven't changed much since my time at St. Thomas More forty years ago. In describing St. Michael's University, they clarify what they mean by the "united endeavour of intelligence and faith." It is a commitment "to the study of the Christian tradition within a context of faith and to fostering the creative engagement of that tradition with the widest range of academic disciplines as well as with other traditions both religious and secular."

What I do know is that in my time as an undergraduate, the Basilians at St. Thomas More lived up to their ideal of fostering creative engagement of the Christian tradition with the history of philosophy.

In class after class, we were taught to be open of mind, within reason, and tolerant in manner — to the extent that Christ's teachings allowed — as we read our way through all the major works from Plato to Nietzsche. We were encouraged to cultivate Aristotle's wide-ranging intellectual curiosity and consider any and all theories, including those of Aristotle, Aquinas, Marx, and Darwin, as tentative. The Basilian Order, through its sponsorship of the world-famous Pontifical Institute of Mediaeval Studies at St. Michael's, saw itself as the principal and most highly principled proponent of Thomism, St. Thomas Aquinas's thirteenth-century modification of Aristotle. The Basilians who taught my generation believed that Thomism could happily and harmoniously reconcile reason and revelation in every case that would ever present itself to students of philosophy. Their unrestrained confidence in the genius of Aquinas allowed them to take intellectual risks and expose us to heterodox thinkers. And as anyone who has ever listened to the marvellous Father Own Lee discuss Wagner on Texaco Metropolitan Opera broadcasts knows, they found their own stylish way of doing it themselves.

Were these priest-professors foolhardy to encourage us to read everything relevant to whatever attracted our interest, so long as we tested what we read against the facts of experience? Were they foolhardy to encourage us to see ourselves as able to understand Western civilization in its roots and branches and to creatively engage with it at its highest levels? Do Basilian educators still challenge first-year students (as they challenged us) to read Augustine's *City of God* and John Henry Cardinal Newman's *The Idea of a University* as extracurricular material for informal discussion? Do they still encourage would-be teachers to read Rousseau's *Confessions* in order to better understand his *Émile* to get at the underlying assumptions of modern philosophies of education? The Basilian fathers provided such enthralling and invigorating adventures in learning that on some days the classroom atmosphere was so charged that I could even forgive my

Campion College teachers the deadly drudgery they'd laid on me. They'd gotten me into St. Thomas More, and there was no place I liked better. Even so, I wasn't necessarily absorbing the best my professors could offer. According to my friend Robert Louis, a Campion classmate, who was pursuing a degree in French literature, you had to read and discuss Montaigne, Voltaire, and Rousseau in the original, not in translation, with Basilians who had lived in France to feel the full effect of their learning and culture. I don't know about that, but I do know that our professors saw Canada as more deeply bilingual and bicultural than most of their contemporaries. They brought both Claude Ryan and Gerard Pelletier to Saskatoon to explain Quebec and its Quiet Revolution to us. If nothing else (and oh, there was so much else), they equipped hundreds like me to fully appreciate the great and greatly under-appreciated novelist and short story writer Hugh Hood when he emerged in full flower later in the decade. You have only to read an essay such as "The Intuition of Being: Morley, Marshall and Me" in Hood's *Unsupported Assertions* (1991) to begin to understand that there is such a thing as a Catholic literary tradition in English Canada and to recognize how central the Basilians and St. Michael's were to forming Morley Callaghan, Marshall McLuhan, and Hugh Hood.

Back at the seminary, Dr. B. tutored me on the connections between philosophy and theology. I hummed with intellectual vitality. Father Jim applauded and offered encouragement. He saw me going places in the church, helping to shape its future in Canada. To get there, I'd have to survive four years of theological studies. Theoretically, the archbishop could send me any number of places, but Father Jim was pretty certain I'd be sent to St. Paul's Seminary in Ottawa, the place from which he'd just graduated. He thought I would do well there as long as I steered clear of the incumbent Rector — a hard man who had almost made it to the National League with a wicked forkball. Seminarians called him Raspberry, and he controlled St. Paul's like he once held the mound; those under his command proceeded through theological training like base runners. You moved at his pace and pleasure. Nobody went after the long ball. Nobody made him look bad. If you crowded him, he dusted you off. If you hot-dogged, he struck you out.

Knowing of my difficult relationship with his predecessor, Father Jim sensed that my ass might be in a sling in my first week in Ottawa and I could be out of the game by Christmas. He thought of a rain delay: if I could get straight A's in my final year, maybe he could persuade my archbishop to let me stay another year in Saskatoon and take an honours degree in philosophy before tackling a degree in theology. Raspberry was scheduled to retire in a year. The prospect delighted me. The University of Saskatchewan had recently hired a former advisor to the Dalai Lama to form a department of far eastern studies, and I wanted to study Buddhism and yoga. I did my part; I ended a rich but exhausting school year with straight A's (a previously unheard of excess of academic achievement at St. Pius X that was soon duplicated by others) and was deflated when the archbishop insisted I start theology studies in Ottawa in September. I was also filled with a deepening anxiety about American nuclear power and foreign policy in southeast Asia. I longed to get back the clarity of mind I'd experienced when I'd first decided I wanted to become a Trappist monk.

After living frugally all summer, I took a wildly circuitous trip to Ottawa in the fall. My books and clerical clothes went east by train, and I crossed the Saskatchewan — Montana border on a Greyhound bus. I took along George Grant's *Lament for a Nation* and Kerouac's *On the Road*. Giving myself ten days to get to Ottawa via Chicago, Detroit, and Toronto, I hadn't said anything to anybody, but I had two other things in mind. One was to hear Miles Davis in Chicago; I'd read in *Downbeat* that his quintet was at the Blackhawk, and I was determined to hear him. I was going to do that and go to some blues clubs, and then I was going to take a bus to Kentucky and go to Gethsemani and talk to Thomas Merton. I figured I stood a good chance of getting to speak with him, since he was Master of Novices at the monastery and one of the people who decided who got accepted. If I did get to speak with him, I knew what I wanted to say. Many magazine and newspaper editors had formed the opinion that Thomas Merton could write on almost any subject, and he had great difficulty turning down any request, judging from the sheer bulk of material being published under his name. I assumed that he could do with some secretarial help. I wasn't the world's best typist, but I was an above-average researcher and could work a mimeograph machine. This last was an important point. Thomas Merton had started circulating copies of his more controversial works as *samizdat*. He'd find me a willing helper if they allowed me to stay at the monastery. It was a confused and ambiguous plan which perfectly reflected the state of my anxieties.

What did I want for myself? I wanted most of all to learn from Tom Merton how to see the difference between those things that concentrated a person on a search for the true self and those things that distorted and destroyed an authentic sense of self, to know which rules to follow and which to break in living a non-materialistic life. Of all the spiritual writers I was reading at the time who weren't Zen Buddhists, Merton seemed to have the surest grasp of matters of personal conscience. I was certain that he was scrupulous in practising what he preached and that if I learned to be spiritual under his care, he'd never usurp my right to make my own decisions. Merton had written extensively about the religious life and the particularities of the monastic life in a series of books that I'd found uneven, sometimes contradictory and annoyingly pious, but flashing with moments of pure brilliance. In writing about the Shakers, for instance, he had written that, facing their own extinction, they had refused to consider that they'd been a failure. Whatever else could be said of them, they knew that they'd stood as a sign, a mystery of purity and goodness in the face of absurdity, absolutely loyal to their vision. He'd written that in the fate of the Shakers we could see that the world and time are a dance of the Lord in emptiness. Merton asserted that if we responded to this phenomenon by over-analyzing things into the strange finalities and complex purposes asserted by Thomistic theology, we'd fall victim to a sadness, absurdity, and despair of our own manufacture. Such despair did not alter the reality of things: the cosmic dance was always there. We had to invite ourselves to forget our purposes and join the dance. The Shakers had expressed the best in the Christian spirit — simplicity, practicality, earnestness, hope — and consequently saw deceptiveness in the secular dream of America, saw that you couldn't build a paradise on the slaughter of Indians and the enslavement of blacks. What a human being really needs is a chance to help himself, an increase in self respect. I could see Merton hadn't resolved all the tensions in his life by becoming a monk. But I also saw that he had what I most lacked, an ambivalence about his life that allowed him to recall his past with both pleasure and pain. I'd rather fail with him than succeed in mastering Raspberry's strike zone up in Ottawa. And so I was on the road to Kentucky, and I was going to dance in Chicago.

No, I wasn't. Riot cops with shields and long sticks and heavy weapons blocked all the exits from the Chicago bus terminal the Sunday night I arrived. They forbade me to leave the building because black people were on a rampage and headed downtown. I must stay inside and take a bus straight out of the city. I went to buy a ticket for Kentucky. A plainclothes cop stepped in front of me.

"Why do you want to go to Kentucky?"

"To see a priest."

"Who are you?"

"I'm a Catholic seminarian from Canada."

"You can't go."

"Why not?"

"They've had enough northern white boys sticking their noses in where they ain't wanted down south."

"That's not why I want to go to Kentucky."

"You're getting on a bus going north. Right now."

And so I did. I was one of only two white passengers, and the white driver made us sit right up behind him. The rest of the bus was full of music, sweet-smelling smoke, and jive talk, and I travelled wide awake through a strange and haunting night to Detroit with a student from Smith College clinging to me for protection.

THIRTEEN

Main Street, Ottawa

St. Paul's Seminary, one of three large buildings belonging to the Oblate order on Main Street in Ottawa, was filled to capacity when I arrived in September 1965. There were about two hundred of us in the residence; another building, linked by a tunnel, held St. Paul's University class-rooms, theatres, and library. A third building, much older and set back further from the street, was an Oblate residence and novitiate. We came from Newfoundland, Nova Scotia, Prince Edward Island, rural Quebec, northern Ontario, Vermont, Rhode Island, Massachusetts, Kansas, Manitoba, Saskatchewan, Alberta, British Columbia, and Sri Lanka. There were unilingual English, unilingual French, Polish-Ameri-cans who waved both nations' flags fiercely, and Franco-Americans who weren't sure which side dominated. Some of the Newfoundlanders were rooted in traditions that predated nation-states by a couple of centuries and expressed themselves in a form of English unintelligible to the rest of us — "gaiters" for overshoes, "cuffs" for mittens, "empt" for pouring tea into a cup. Some of the Americans had been in semi-naries since the age of twelve and knew no other life; others had been all over the world with the US army, navy or air force; many had come to St. Paul's as first-year philosophy students and were entwined in the lore of the place and purveyors of its legends. Only a couple dozen of us were newcomers — about as many as those who were fluently bilingual.

One thing we had in common: we'd been judged by our bishops to be bright enough to train for the priesthood at St. Paul's Pontifical University, which had a reputation as one of the more intellectually challenging academies of philosophy, theology, canon law, and scripture studies in Catholic North America. Most days, that sense of our own brilliance was about all we had in common. We were contentious, argumentative, quarrelsome, capable of disagreeing over anything from minor points of social decorum to essential theological principles. Everything was at issue among us, and if there were six, sixteen, or sixty-four sides to an issue, we were sure to find them all. Those who agreed on one thing were at loggerheads over another within five minutes. It made for fluid and flexible relationships and a social life that lurched between moments when all individuality ceased to matter and other times of terrible aloneness. During recreation periods, we were caustic and cynical, uncharitable in our gossip, and constantly gossiping, as vile as teenaged girls. But we rarely lied. We simply knew when to be economical with the truth. According to principles of Catholic moral theology, a lie is always a lie, but some are "profitable" and others are "harmful," depending on whether they benefit the liar without injuring others. Profitable lies are either insincere or hypocritical; in either case, they're considered minor faults, venial sins. Some of the Americans had good reason to become master economists with the truth and exceedingly careful about what they said. Getting turfed from the seminary meant losing their draft deferments. And that, in most cases, meant immediate call-up for service in Vietnam.

It soon became clear to me that there were several different kinds of priests-in-the-making at St. Paul's. The most obvious were flashers, young men of ambition eager to consort with anyone they thought might one day advance their careers. Cautious on every issue and much given to sucking up to authorities by spying on the rest of us, they seemed to have no interests outside the church and were obsessed with public image, charm-school manners, and attending formal receptions at various embassies, especially the American. The porkers, swinishly indolent permanent adolescents, figured that the priesthood was a sinecure of minimal work and maximum gain, particularly in girth; they organized their scholarly obligations so that the need to pass examinations inconvenienced them little as possible. Thanks to their ingenuity, anybody willing to pay their inflated prices had access to typed and mimeoed study notes for every course, as well as copies of exams and tests from previous years. The boy scouts among us were very effective men, fearless leaders good at doing the right thing without necessarily attracting attention for it. Holy Joes were weird and skewed, out on the edge, seeking sainthood. I wasn't sure where — if anywhere — I fit in. Like all newcomers, I was nicknamed within a week of arriving and pigeonholed: I was Fritz the Cat, because I never came when I was called and disliked those who most wanted me to like them.

It was easier to live with the insincerity of some of the American seminarians than the hypocrisy of others. It was one thing to not openly oppose the Asian war, it was quite another to be loudly in favour of it. On November 11, 1965, during his lunch hour, Roger Lapointe set fire to himself in front of the United Nations building in New York by pouring lighter fluid over his hair and clothing and igniting it; he wanted to express the full horror of what American troops were doing in Vietnam with napalm raids against villages and their inhabitants. Lapointe was a Catholic socialist on the staff of *The Catholic Worker* and a member of Tom and Daniel Berrigan's Catholic Peace Fellowship. His self-immolation caused great consternation near the end of my first semester. To a majority at St. Paul's, Lapointe's act was either lunacy or grievous sin. To a few of us, such self-slaughter bore witness to an existential crisis none of us was in any position to judge. Are people who foresee genocide and act it out more highly attuned to the human condition than others easily comprehend? What is the difference between a death wish induced by crimes of public leaders and a private neurosis? What is sanity in an insane world? If you can't ask such questions, how deeply can you hope to see into the twentieth century? A lot of our fellow seminarians saw me and these others as lacking true faith just for speculating about such things.

Over the next eighteen months, I discovered the limits of my own faith. At first, I was riding an emotional roller coaster and was more than a tad self-absorbed with other issues. After sixteen years as a model nun and a role model to me, my second-oldest sister left her convent to marry a teacher from Campion who was three-quarters of the way to becoming a Jesuit. One high-school friend died in a boating accident; another was killed when he drove his motorcycle under a trailer truck. The two seminarians who were my best friends at St. Paul's dropped out before the first year was over, leaving a big hole behind them. Unlike them, I didn't feel myself so hormonally driven to distraction by women that life in leisure hours had come down to one set of alternatives — get laid or get drunk. Liquor was quicker, less expensive, less "deadly" a sin than satisfying lust in a brothel in Hull or with a blow job from a streetwalker in the Byward Market, but both my friends had family histories of alcoholism and feared becoming "plastered saints" — the category of seminarians and priests that cut across all other boundaries. I had fewer fears and more self-control when it came to drinking than they did, but I was far more addled and raddled about my sexuality in the overheated atmosphere of that seminary residence.

My own sexual preferences were well defined. Like my two friends and most heterosexual males of that age, I could fall into all sorts of involuntary erotic responses and become mildly unfocused by sudden flashes of human flesh, especially female cleavages fore and aft. But serious lust, the thing of wet dreams and mortal sins that caused me to forget time and consequences, was reserved for petite women, stylishly dressed, with clean, healthy hair that looked its natural colour even if it wasn't and shapely legs that terminated in smallish feet. And good skin. And powerful, probing blue or green eyes. And cultivated voices that spoke a lightly accented English free of my own mid-western twang. The voice, always her voice, was the clincher. Your guess is as good as Sigmund Freud's or Steven Pinker's as to which events between conception and puberty left me so particularly narrow-banded in my sexual hardwiring. At the same time, I discovered myself to be erotically colour-blind. I found (and find) women of every complexion and colouration attractive. To keep cool and free of serious temptation, I told myself I only had to avoid French supper clubs on the Hull side of the river, refuse invitations to foreign embassy receptions, drink in bars that had exclusively male staff, walk quickly through the Byward Market, and not get into conversations with the females at the National Gallery's information desk. When we had free time and were allowed to go into town or out on the town, the National Gallery gave me the most trouble. I was drawn to contemporary Canadian painting just then, but to get to that gallery I had to pass a desk that always seemed to be staffed by a woman who could have been the younger sister of Helene at the Modern Times Bookstore back in Regina. She too had a thing about poetry — a copy of Leonard Cohen's *Spice Box of Earth* sat on the desk whenever she was on duty. What I had no control over was who was attracted to me.

From my days as a paper boy, I'd always had sweet and gentle friends who weren't attracted to girls but were interested in talking to me about what clothes to buy and how to wear them or about flowers or music or poetry or foreign films or Oscar Wilde, but feelings beyond comradeship were never expressed. Neither they nor I wanted to be labelled "queer" at a high school and in a city where homophobic bullying was rampant and all too readily accepted by too many teachers and school administrators. At St. Paul's, seminarians were formally warned by the Rector against forming "particular friendships" —

spending too much time in the company of any one person to the exclusion of others. We were to do everything in threesomes or larger groups. An all-male *menage à trois* was outside his imaginative grasp, I guess. Everyone knew that overt homosexual acts could be punished by immediate expulsion. Even so, a few seminarians weren't circumspect about their attraction to other men. They found things to do in small groups that seemed innocuous but provided lots of opportunities for pairings and privacy. The Museum of Natural History was one trysting place. A health and fitness club was another. A group that went on excursions to study the architecture and furnishings of local churches was also reputed to be inordinately fond of Judy Garland movies and wearing women's silk underwear. I'd gone to the health club in innocence, persuaded that taking a sauna was a great way to relax. It was, until I was propositioned, not by a brother seminarian or priest, but by an army officer. He left me in no doubt as to what he wanted to do to me and what he wanted me to do to him in return, which pretty much answered any questions I'd ever had about the mechanics of homosexual couplings and the erotic uses of a swagger stick. Being lewdly approached on my second visit to the sauna in my first year in Ottawa upset me to a disproportionate degree. I began to ask myself in the small hours of the night whether other older men were attracted to me for the same reason without my realizing it. The question was important because I'd generally assumed that nice, helpful, generous older men, such as the visiting priest from Regina who extolled the benefits of saunas and introduced me to that particular health club, had only my best interests at heart. It's an assumption a lot of boys who have lost their fathers at an early age make about the adult male world.

While I was worrying about the men, mostly priests, who had befriended me during my adolescence and coming to manhood, a seminarian of my own age made it all too clear that he had fallen in love with me. He took it badly when I repelled his advances in a casually brutish way. He was given to dramatic gestures and did some foolish things that left him no alternative but to leave St. Paul's before he was expelled. Dazed, I went to see my spiritual director to tell him that I was going home at Christmas and not returning.

At Saskatoon, we'd had no choice in spiritual directors. Dr. B. had looked after the otherworldly welfare of everyone. At St. Paul's, we could choose any one of a dozen priests in residence. Father Jim steered me towards his own former director, Père Rosaire, and it was a agreeable matchup. My new spiritual director heard my confession every week, but he heard it in his study, not in a black box, and instead of simply reciting sins, I had to speak openly and truthfully about the vices I was attempting to overcome and the virtues I was struggling to acquire. Père Rosaire was a European-trained philosopher who had spent much of his time in graduate school thinking about the Christian virtues of faith, hope, and charity, and the classic virtues of prudence, justice, fortitude, and temperance, and how they might be exercised in the world of Sartre, Camus, and Heidegger. An elegant man of refined tastes, he encouraged me to spend more of my time listening to Bach and Mozart and less listening to the racket inside my head. The more I understood their music, the better I'd understand myself. It was a good prescription. I heeded it. He also recommended that I take my sexual concerns to a lay analyst and stay in the seminary until I'd figured out who I was and what I most wanted to do with my life. In the meantime, he ran interference between Raspberry and me. With remarkable patience, grace, tact, and humour, Père Rosaire led me to see that my problems with people in authority, my perplexities about my father's death, and my conflicts with myself all had to be dealt with in a psychotherapeutic way on somebody else's time. When we talked, we talked about issues we had with our church, and especially which ones were being addressed and which avoided at the Second Vatican Council. We had more than enough to keep us talking all year.

There hadn't been a general council of the church since the nineteenth century, when a deeply divided Vatican I had declared the

Pope to be infallible in matters of faith and morals. Infallible or not, the line of popes from Pius IX through Pius XII ratcheted Vatican autocracy and totalitarianism tighter and tighter. Before the bishops of the world sat down to the first meeting of Vatican II in the fall of 1962, pre-conciliar documents were prepared by international commissions controlled from the curia, the Vatican bureaucracy. All the bureaucrats, most of the bishops, and the majority of interested bystanders presumed that after an interval of preening by the more grandiloquent among the princes of the church, a few minor modifications would be made and approval would be unanimous. The main outcome would be photo opportunities for a Roman Catholic Church that was more flamboyant than the British monarchy and as much given to triumphal parades of power as the Kremlin on May Day. This council would be over by Christmas 1962, and that would be that for another century or so, as far as gestures towards Catholic democracy might go. In his opening remarks, John XXIII had thrown a wild pitch by telling the bishops that it was their job to express the beliefs of their church in the language of the times, to express hope in a dark age by giving new life to their communities. It provoked a *crise de conscience*: an infallible Pope had told his church to stop being such a failure. The church, he said, had to break out of the palaces in which it had institutionalized itself, end its narcissistic ways, start putting service to humanity ahead of self-interest. Even though he knew that many bishops thought as he did, they wanted him to change what needed to be changed on his own initiative. And if he did, nothing essential would alter. He would merely have concentrated more power in the papacy. To achieve meaningful changes, the bishops had to reassert their role as successors of the apostles. It was up to the bishops themselves to run the council. That was what John XXIII told them. This led to calls for an immediate postponement by some bishops, and the curia started to lose its grip on the proceedings. New commissions were struck and the precon-ciliar documents were rewritten; the sourest Vatican vinegars drained away, and both old and new wines were funnelled into new and old bottles.

The Second Vatican Council met in four sessions. The first session opened, with those papal pronouncements, on October 11, 1962, and closed on December 8 of the same year. Pope John XXIII, whose idea the council was, died on June 3, 1963, expressing the hope that he would watch its continuation from Heaven. His successor, Paul VI, called for the second session to begin on September 29, 1963, and it ran until December 4, 1963. The third session was held from September 14 to November 21, 1964. The fourth and final session ran from September 14 to December 8, 1965. Entering St. Pius X just weeks before the council opened and leaving St. Paul's sixteen months after it ended, I was a seminarian through all of it. But all of what, exactly? A great deal of nonsense was written at the time and long afterwards about what happened then and there. The most widely disseminated mythic version among Catholics can be summed up, more or less, as follows: the Second Vatican Council was the first church council that did not meet to combat a schism or heresy, and in the absence of external enemies and threats, it took on a wholly unpredictable life of its own. Miraculously recognizing that it was the will of God, a providential event made manifest through the Holy Spirit in the person of John XXIII, for the church to urgently pursue Christian unity by renovating its evangelical presence in the world, sincere and prolonged discussions between liberal and conservative groups gave rise to compromises that so reflected the general will of the church that they were passed by huge majorities and then implemented with deference to local conditions as a preparation for its second millennium. That's certainly the interpretation of Vatican II articulated by John Paul II in his public utterances, but it also runs through his predecessors right back to John XXIII, who believed the council would become "a new Pentecost." This myth, like all good archetypal stories, can be told several different ways — the conservatives can be drawn as more or less intransigent, the liberals as more or less open-minded, and either side painted black or white. A complete counter-myth is also possible; some see Vatican II as the work of Satan and a heretical John XXIII and condemn it as such on their websites. What actually happened?

At the time the council was meeting in its various sessions, the most intriguing reports of what was going on were those that appeared as "Letters from Vatican City" in *The New Yorker* under the pseudonymous byline of "Xavier Rynne." Rynne, who was later identified as Father Francis X. Murphy, a Redemptorist priest, was very chatty, so much so that his reports were later compiled into four books. Rynne saw the council in institutional and bureaucratic terms as a tug-of-war over turf fought by two gangs of clerics — the devious reactionaries led by Alfredo Cardinal Ottaviani, who controlled the curia, and the open-minded forces of desirable change led by Augustin Cardinal Bea, who had the support of John XXIII and the majority of bishops. Prior to Rynne's reports, factionalism in the church was glossed over rather than detailed. Rynne can be credited with taking the terms "liberal" and "conservative" from American political life and applying them, more or less intact, to the religious arena of the council. This transfer of terminology has caused more than a little mischief. In the world of Catholicism, differences between liberals and conservatives are a perennial feature of discussions, secular and sacred, and have much more to do with mood than motives. Liberalism, as Europeans and Canadians generally understand it, is a political ideal which promotes pluralism as a virtue in itself, and defends as many kinds of thinking and acting within a population as can be accommodated without social anarchy. As such, it has never been part of the Roman Catholic Church. Catholicism has never seen any virtue in uncertainty. At St. Paul's, those who tutored us in the art of preparing sermons and delivering them had no tolerance for qualifiers and disclaimers: we were coached never to give way to nervousness, never to project any form of doubt.

As Terry Eagleton, one of the English academic world's more notorious cultural theorists, remarks in *The Gatekeeper,* his own lively memoir of growing up Catholic in England: "One can move fairly freely, then, from Catholicism to Marxism without having to pass through liberalism. The path from the Tridentine creed to Trotskyism is shorter than it seems."

The mood of the first session was very mixed and full of dramatic shift. Ottaviani and Guiseppi Cardinal Siri and their chief American allies, Francis Cardinal Spellman of New York and James Cardinal McIntyre of Los Angeles, were chased from centre stage as bishops from north of the Alps and their Third World allies coalesced into the party of John XXIII. The real conflict of Vatican II became apparent only at the third and final session in 1965. The battle line was drawn not between liberal and conservative forces, but between "traditionalists," who wanted to maintain the church as an exclusive and closed fortress, and "innovators," who envisioned an inclusive church based on the principle that "he who is not against us is with us." The conflict was no longer a question of how much the church would reform itself but whether or not it could change anything more substantial than its forms of public worship.

During the first session, the traditionalists, led by Ottaviani — whose motto was *Semper idem,* "always the same" — were blindsided by John XXIII and the coalition of bishops Bea had rallied around him. Caught off-guard, the curialed oligarchy short-circuited what was threatening to become an anarchic process by resorting to obfuscation, delay, and character assassination during the discussions on liturgical reform and the use of the vernacular. Even so, they surrendered more ground than they ever imagined they would when the bishops opted for the vernacular in worship, because Latin was their principal instrument of hegemony. It took the second session to restore traditionalist self-confidence. In the meetings that began on September 2, 1964, Ottaviani's oligarchs showed they were back in power, flexing their muscles in the discussions on the place of the church in the world. While the bishops were studying the statement concerning the Jewish people that had been John XXIII's special project, there was an anonymous distribution of anti-Semitic hate literature, including copies of that notorious old forgery *The Protocols of the Elders of Zion*. Meant as a warning shot, it had its effect. Rather than provoke an incident within the council by insisting on a full and fervent apology to all the Jewish people, living and dead, that might spill over into the larger arena of Arab-Israeli relations, the party of innovation accepted the compromises they were offered: traditionalist documents that continue to offend Jews and Buddhists thirty years later, and, in particular, a document of episcopal collegiality that looked good but lacked substance.

Vatican II had been a constant and rich topic of discussion, gossip, and debate at St. Pius X thanks to Dr. B. and Father Jim. In Ottawa, the council was discussed with more heat and far less enlightenment. St. Paul's was in the business of training elite priests who would be useful to their bishops as canon lawyers, theological advisers, religious education teachers. Acquiring priestly skills and competency in their application were far more important to most of the students than satisfying intellectual curiosity. The pre-Vatican II church in which we'd been raised and in which the majority still wanted to live was a very comfortable cocoon, with clear caste boundaries between communities of priests, nuns, and the laity. The most prized skill was mastery of the priestly mystique, the ability to project holiness and other-worldliness while controlling the many levers that kept a parish — a complex plant with buildings, employees, capital and operating budgets, and so many other things — delivering a full-service spiritual system. But the more I and a few like-minded, left-leaning seminarians looked at Vatican II and studied the sixteen documents it produced, the more we began to see that the system itself was based on a denial of history, a denigration of women, and an embarrassing insistence on a deeply flawed understanding of biology and cosmology. The more I came to understand this, the less willing I was to buy into the myth of the council in any of its narratives. Having grown up in Saskatchewan during the CCF years, I'd learned that the only political terms that really matter in any public debate are the ancient ones of right and left: to the right, the rulers, the top dogs; to the left, the workers, the underdogs. The Roman palace is on the right; the Christian arena is on the left.

At St. Paul's, formal classes in anything other than church history or Bible study bored me. Rather than doze through them, I played rubber upon rubber of bridge with other slackers who became as dependent as I did on the course notes we bought from the fattest seminarian on the premises. When the cards weren't running right, I went to the wonderful St. Paul's research library and read books and articles outside the curriculum that interested me, topics to fuel my weekly discussions with Père Rosaire and his successor. Talking with Père Rosaire about Johann Sebastian Bach's *Mass in B Minor* set me thinking about the ways in which a Lutheran Mass differs from a Catholic one. And that led to reading a then-new English edition of the collected works of Martin Luther. The more I read Luther's own words, the more I sensed that he had gotten it right in his protests and reforms: the church of his time had lost its way and fallen into darkness. Despite a Counter-Reformation and the best efforts of Vatican II, the church still couldn't see the way to reform as clearly as Luther had because Vatican II could not openly debate Luther's contention that a priesthood that had celibacy imposed upon it would always be a defective and deficient priesthood which disabled and diminished at least as many as it enabled and magnified. The evidence of that was all around me. I could see it in others, but I couldn't see it in myself, not with any clarity. Despite my weekly sessions with a pretty good psychologist, I wasn't making many advances towards an understanding of my own sexuality.

It was only when a mock examination question on the nature of God stared me in the face as I studied for my final exams that I clearly realized that I was no longer a true believer. In fact, I began to wonder if

I was any kind of a believer at all. This was in the days of "God Is Dead" theology, when a few American theologians were deriving inspiration from Nietzsche's parable of the madman who ran through the market shouting that mankind had killed God. I'd been reading Nietzsche closely. I'd also been studying the Big Bang theory and could see that if the universe self-assembles and self-destructs, given enough time, there was no way to figure out what happened. Ever. If God could not be seen to exist, He could not be said to exist in any rational way. I saw that the end of rational belief was the end of natural theology and the end of Catholicism as a unique form of Christianity. Without a God who was knowable, my knowledge and skills as a priest were worthless. And me, what was I worth as anything other than a Catholic priest? After five years of seminary life, I felt very worthless. Then I failed my final exams for my BTh, the degree that would allow me to progress to my final two years in the seminary and ordination into the priesthood.

FOURTEEN

Kitchen Tales

Shortly after the term at St. Paul's started in the autumn of 1965, every first year student in the theology program was provided with a list of fifty theses. Theses were statements of major questions that had faced the church through its first two millennia. Some were little changed from the time of Aquinas; some had been shaped by the Counter-Reformation's Council of Trent and others by the First Vatican Council's quarrels with more modern thinkers. The theory of education that shaped priests between the two Vatican councils was that theology may be well done or poorly done, learned or common, well informed by true scholarship or ill-performed by base thinkers, smart or dumb, but it was either true or heretical — that was the key point. The point to studying theses was to inform oneself of where the truth was to be found in the teachings of the church and how to learn how to restate it in ways that avoided any hint of the heresies lurking in the background. You did this by memorizing which passages in the Old Testament had been used by New Testament writers to support their claims that Jesus was Christ, what New Testament verses and citations of Greek philosophy had been used by Augustine, Aquinas, other approved thinkers, and church councils to support which papal teachings, and then by mastering the arguments that linked the quotations one to another. At the end of two years, you were expected to enter an examination hall where three slips of paper would be picked from a hat like raffle tickets, and the theses on these slips were written out on the blackboard. You chose one of the three and wrote your response to it in three or four hours. If what you wrote was not poorly done, not unscholarly, not ill-informed, not dumb, and utterly free of heresy, you were given an appointment for an oral examination by a tribunal of professors who would question you on as many or as few of the remaining theses as could be crammed into fifteen minutes or so. If you passed that inspection, you could proceed to two more years of studying more theses, another such exam, the signing of an oath against ever holding or promoting a number of specific modern heresies, and then you'd be ordained to the priesthood. The courses offered at St. Paul's University were dual purpose: they provided the background knowledge and skills necessary to succeed in the written and oral exams, and they gave a more practical training in preaching, teaching, and enforcing church doctrines. In my two years there, I followed courses sporadically — attendance wasn't compulsory, and quite a few of us preferred bridge, chess, snooker, snoozing, or even private study — on church doctrines regarding God, revelation, creation, grace, and salvation, as well as practical ones in Biblical languages — Greek and Hebrew — and canon law. I showed up on time with my mind fully engaged only for the classes in Biblical studies and church history.

By the time I arrived at St. Paul's, Vatican II had already made some impact on the curriculum. Latin had been dropped as the required language of instruction, and every course was available in either French or English. While a few professors continued to do much as they had always done and gave back to us precisely what had been given to them in their student days, the others brought the documents and debates of

Vatican II into the classrooms. The most dramatic impact of the council, however, was felt in a more ordinary and immediate way: discipline was relaxed. In the first year, we were allowed to go into downtown Ottawa or Hull on Saturday nights for restaurant meals and movies once we'd secured the Rector's permission. If you missed the eleven PM curfew, you came up the fire escape and risked getting caught and having the privilege suspended. In the second year, Père Rosaire replaced Raspberry as Rector, and we could come and go as we pleased all weekend through an unlocked door. All we had to do was signal in advance which meals we'd be taking in residence so that enough food would be prepared and none wasted. The seminary exploded with new activities. Those who could afford it went skiing or spent weekends on the town in Montreal. With all this going on, my failure of my final exams caused more of a flutter than my dropping out and leaving did. I was one of the ones expected to do brilliantly on the exams. I spent the night before the final in the restaurant and bar of the Chateau Laurier with the two friends who'd replaced the ones I'd lost a year earlier. We ate steak, drank doubles of Johnny Walker, smoked Havana cigars, and got maudlin listening to a pretty good torch singer. I have no idea what I wrote the next morning. It was quickly dismissed as poorly done, unscholarly, ill-informed, and too dumb to be ruled heretical. Père Rosaire delivered that verdict in person. He thought I was suffering from exhaustion. I was certainly badly hung over. I went to bed and slept for twenty hours. After I woke up and packed my bags, I told my drinking companions and a couple of other friends I was leaving. Their general assumption was that it had everything to do with sex and not much to do with anything else. It was getting to be a bit of a trend: they knew my sister had left the convent to get married the previous year, and closer to hand, one of my favourite bridge partners had been informed in a very public way that he was going to become a father a couple of years before he was scheduled to be ordained. A very pregnant young woman he'd worked alongside at a summer camp arrived at the seminary with her parents and blindsided the father-to-be as we filed out of chapel on our way to our midday meal.

Returning just long enough the following September to re-sit the exams I'd failed, I resolutely turned my back on that place and the people I'd known there. After I'd said goodbye to my friends and had a long conversation with Père Rosaire, I went downtown and bought a train ticket back to Regina. Then I hailed a cab to Rockcliffe and went down to the water's edge and slowly and deliberately pissed in the river. Sometimes it feels really good to actually piss on something, it always feels wonderful to piss into flowing water, and I went to the river and pissed in it to show my contempt for the loss of will I'd experienced during my final weeks in the seminary and to exult in a newly dis-covered joy in being alive. I walked back to the Chateau Laurier and smoked the last Cuban cigar I could afford to buy until I'd earned some money. Sometimes I still wake in the middle of the night with the taste of it on my tongue, the smell of its curling smoke in my nostrils. It was fine Havana leaf, hand-rolled, a cigar worth remembering. Smoking it, I knew I'd freed myself from any further temptation to suicide. Agnos-ticism wasn't taboo outside the seminary, and my life was back in my own hands. For five years, I'd let others rule me and had accepted the harsh disciplining of my sexuality and everything else those seminaries had imposed because Father Walt insisted I had a calling to the priesthood and I was willing to take the chance that he was right and act against self-interest. With a lot of help from the philosophy of Thomas Aquinas, I'd persuaded myself that what I was doing was enlightened, that there was intense illumination to be found in the pre-Reformation church, that the connection between reason and revelation was precisely what my Basilian teachers made it out to be: a union of intelligence and faith that enabled people to realize the full measure of their humanity. Studying the Bible and the history of the church at St. Paul's changed my view of the priesthood to something very Lutheran. Studying

Nietzsche alone in my seminary cell changed my views of reason and Christian revelation. My vocation and my faith were both dead. I buried them both with a piss and a smoke and walked away.

When I wrote *A Blue Boy in a Black Dress*, I didn't provide even this much of the story of those five years in the seminary. I could have written of them by the yard, following the trail of my diminishing faith book by book along my shelves, in one room after another, from Saskatoon through my Ottawa sojourn, obsessively piling one distressing memory on top of the other. I didn't do it partly because I didn't want to drive my readers to distraction, but mostly because I thought I'd provided enough evidence to make a more general point about those of us who were Catholics when the church collapsed as a moral and intellectual, social and personal, ritual and aesthetic framework in which it was possible to live a whole — if not always wholesome — life. That point was, and is, that we have learned to live with cognitive dissonance: what we most expected has not transpired, and what we never anticipated has come to pass. Hellfire and brimstone have not rained down upon us, and some of us have actually come to accept and love our own bodies. We are less cursed and more blessed than we'd ever been taught to imagine. We are people of unanswered prayers, more like former Communist Party members in, say, Germany since re-unification than the mass media ever recognize. Until recently, this satisfied me as a reasonably complete explanation for why I entered the seminary and why I left the church.

On January 27, 2003, I had a stroke — a cerebral hemorrhage in the part of the brain that controls the lower right side of the body. I didn't know that was what was happening to me. It was a Monday — the non-teaching day in my work week — and I'd done as I usually did in those days: risen early, written for seventy-five minutes before breakfast, worked out in the weight room at my local YMCA, stopped for a coffee, bought some groceries, and returned home. I felt no light-headedness, dizziness, or blurred vision — the usual warning signs. All I noticed was that when I removed my winter boots, my right foot felt as if it had fallen into a very deep sleep. The more I tried to walk it off, the less sensation my foot had. I ignored this and made lunch for myself and my wife, who was due home from work. While we ate, I felt my leg losing sensation more rapidly. When the numbness reached my knee, I said something about it. We went to the neighbourhood walk-in clinic. A young doctor saw me right away, listened to my description of symptoms, tested my right foot for reflex responses. There were none. "You're having a stroke," she said. "We'd better get you to the Royal Victoria Hospital right away. It's attached to the Montreal Neurological Institute." I knew that: I'd seen the walkway between the two on University Avenue. She advised us to take a taxi. "It's much faster than an ambulance," she said. And she gave me a note and phoned the hospital. We took a cab, and it was fast, but it didn't feel fast enough. The loss of sensation was now well above my hip and rising along my right side. In the taxi, my right arm went numb. I thought, "If it reaches my neck, I'm in serious trouble." By the time I'd been rushed through emergency triage and laid on a gurney and manoeuvred into a space in one of the corridors, the numbness had stopped at my shoulder and begun to retreat. My arm felt normal, my side too.

"That was a scary few minutes," I said to my constant companion.

"More like two or three terrifying hours," she said.

The stroke came on the day of the week when I frequently write book reviews. As I lay awake that night on the gurney, still parked in a corridor where the lights never went off, I couldn't compose or recompose a single sentence for the review I'd been writing of Steven Pinker's *Blank Slate: The Modern Denial of Human Nature*. A small vein had ruptured on the left side of my brain and blood seeped into surrounding tissue, and the part of my mind in which I hear as I write no longer functioned. It was as numb and dumb as my reflex-free foot. The silence inside my head was mostly trauma-induced, or so I hoped. I'd had a few very rough hours. I'd faced my possible death and, worse, my fear of paralysis. I still feared permanent diminishment, feared being less than I'd managed to become in my nearly fifty-nine years. By the end of my eighteen-hour stay in hospital under close observation, I knew I'd lost more than the sensation in my lower right leg and foot. Among other collateral damage, my authorial voice had gone missing.

At home, the next day, I was relieved to discover that I could still read — that the stroke hadn't triggered a return to the dyslexia I'd learned to work around in my childhood. But it was disheartening to realize that while I could absorb factual information from the Internet about what a stroke can do to a person's mental functions, I could no longer follow the arguments in Pinker's book, the less dense essays in David Lodge's *Consciousness and the Novel* at my bedside, or even keep the characters and plot of a murder mystery straight in my head. For the first time in my life I had to convalesce without literary company — I could not read for pleasure, I could not write with delight.

Stroke affects people in different ways, depending on the type of stroke, the area of the brain affected, and the extent of the brain injury. Stroke can affect the senses, motor activity, speech, the ability to understand speech, behavioural and thought patterns, memory, and emotions. It can paralyze. Survivors can cry easily, have sudden mood swings for no apparent reason. Depression is common. Stroke survivors feel less than whole because loss of feeling or visual field results in a loss of awareness: we ignore items on our affected side, bumping into furniture or people, and have trouble following instructions on labels and signs in buildings. A stroke can affect touching, moving, and thinking, so a person's perception of everyday objects may be changed. Stroke survivors may not be able to recognize and understand familiar people and objects. Objects may appear closer or farther away than they really are. Spills at the table are common. Survivors may have problems understanding speech, may also have trouble saying what we're thinking. This aphasia affects the ability to talk, listen, read, and write. It's most common when a stroke weakens the body's right side. Stroke can affect the ability to think clearly, can make planning and carrying out even simple activities hard. Survivors may not know how to start a task, confuse the sequence of logical steps in tasks, or forget how to do tasks we've done many times before. I experienced all of these to some degree. Aphasia is the most frightening. The related losses in ability to think clearly and sequentially and increased forgetfulness are the most troubling and most persistent.

But other, positive things happened after my stroke. I was startled to hear music with much greater clarity than I'd heard it in years. My listening ear is suddenly fresh, and old favourites sound new. A stack of jazz CDs that I inherited from my friend Bill, who had died months earlier, and Beethoven string quartets from my own collection got me through the dreadful eyes-wide-open hours that began around midnight and lasted till four in the morning. As I listened once again to the Miles Davis Quintet with John Coltrane, the Gerry Mulligan and Dave Brubeck quartets, Oscar Peterson's trios — all old pals from high school and my summer vacations from the seminary — I started to recollect former times without embarrassment and with extraordinary sensory detail. I found myself looking at black and white photographs of my seminary-era self and not only "seeing " the colours of my clothes but also "feeling" their textures and "touching" the rooms in which I had sat for the camera. I liked the person I found there and wasn't embarrassed by the things he did or the things that had been done to him. I marvelled at how I could have written of him in *A Blue Boy* without saying at least a little of the things that happened to him in the weeks following his departure from St. Paul's.

Back in Regina I took a job at a dairy, doing the hardest physical labour I've ever done for pay. Milk trains still ran then, and I started my day, just after six o'clock, at a railway siding on a loading dock, hauling cream cans inside the dairy from where railway workers had deposited them. After that, it was one tough job after another as I weighed and tested cream, trolleyed it to the mixing room, poured fresh cream and concentrated milk powder into vats, added fresh milk and water according to an easy-to-remember formula, set the mixers running, and took my position on the bottling line until the run was finished. Then, it was on with oilskins and up with brushes, polishing cloths, and fire hoses, and into the vats to scrub them out, and finally collapsing, so tired and worn out that it took a pint of free ice cream to get up enough energy to punch out at three o'clock. The men I worked alongside always headed for a nearby tavern and drank for a couple of hours. I walked home, even though it took the better part of an hour. It was the only time I had to catch some sun, and I needed it. I'd come of age with many too many moles on my face, and once I started shaving, they posed a problem — they were difficult to avoid and easy to cut. I had seven prominent ones removed and a couple of dozen stitches sewn into my face almost as soon as I arrived back in Regina. Since I couldn't do it safely, I didn't shave at all while the incisions closed and healed. I looked like I'd been in a bar fight and had gotten the worst of it. People tended to avert their eyes when they saw me coming along a downtown sidewalk, especially at the end of a mid-afternoon shift, and that pleased me. I didn't want to talk to many people outside my immediate family. I'd returned home mainly to spend some time with my mother and sisters and to make enough money to get myself started at McMaster in clothes that didn't have reminders of the seminary written all over them. The person I least wanted to talk to and avoided completely, never to speak to him again in the rest of his long life, was Father Walt. We'd spoken over the telephone between Ottawa and Regina in the days leading up to my attempt to kill myself and the days leading from that attempt to my exit from the seminary. He'd tried to persuade me several times that he knew me better than I'd ever know myself. I didn't like his tactics one bit. I knew that if I saw him, I'd want to punch him in the mouth for the ways in which he'd tried to alter my decision to leave the seminary by manipulating my emotions. I did attend Sunday Masses at the cathedral, but I didn't take a wafer at the communion rail, and I sat near the back and left the building before he left the altar. A couple of priests who had always taken some interest in me called at my mother's house to see me. One was someone I'm going to call Father Kitchen because that was his favourite room at my mom's and in all the other houses he regularly visited. In retrospect, it amazes me that I wrote *A Blue Boy in a Black Dress* without finding a place to mention him.

I'm tempted to call Kitchen something like Chaosovitch because it rhymes with "son of a bitch," and nearly every priest in the Regina Archdiocese regarded him as an SOB who stirred up confusion wherever he went, but he'd long ago dropped some middle European syllables from his surname. None of the priests I knew admitted to knowing much about who he was or where he'd come from before he arrived in the province and entered the service of the Archdiocese of Regina. Those who did tell stories about him tended to contradict each other. Father Kitchen liked things that way. There was something of the hired gun about him, the stranger in town, the outsider. People used to say that somebody should write a book about him someday, but Kitchen didn't like books very much — he read *Time* and *Life* — and never told me enough about himself that I could be the one to write it. What he did tell me was also so full of mischief that it doesn't seem right to give him the name he used of himself. If this was a film script, I wouldn't need to explain the name switch: changing names is one of the things that scriptwriters do regularly when the credits say "based on a true story."

Kitchen liked movies so much that he made amateur travelogues, and he probably would have suggested casting Clint Eastwood as himself in any feature about his life. What a comic mismatch. Kitchen was short, stocky, unhandsome, and not in the least tight-lipped, except about his own past. Given a chance, he'd spout for hours. Few people gave him the chance. They didn't like to hear what he had to say because he had the bleakest view of the human race most of his audience would ever encounter anywhere outside the criminal justice system or a Samuel Beckett play. He was a firm believer in Original Sin and predestination. Mankind was radically corrupt and depraved. Only God's grace could ever save anyone from the fatal attractions of evil. Unlike Calvinists, he believed that salvation brought no transitory, earthly rewards. What God put into a priest's hands in the way of money must be spent doing what Jesus would do. When I was the kid who played at being Paul Savard, the thing that had fascinated me the most about Father Kitchen was that he owned a genuine cowboy gun, a Colt .45 Peacemaker, and he kept it in easy reach of his car seat until he replaced it with a Smith and Wesson .38 Police Special. He always carried a lot of cash and didn't intend to lose it to any hold-up artist. When I told him I was entering the seminary, he didn't congratulate me like other priests did. Father Kitchen said, "Many are called, few are chosen. It's hell on earth, you know, to be chosen," and mumbled something else between slurps of coffee. He drank a lot of coffee, all of it messily but with great enjoyment. As he drained his cup, he said, "The best reason for doing what has to be done to get to heaven is that you won't find many priests there. And very few bishops. No cardinals, and only the odd Pope."

I laughed. I shouldn't have.

He took my laughter as a sign that I needed an education in priest-craft that no seminary would ever provide. It started with a gift copy of *The Imitation of Christ*, the only religious book he thought worth reading, other than the gospels. "Don't try to do what Jesus did. Don't try to feel what Jesus felt. That's just wacky. You can't fill his shoes. You let him fill yours. When you do as JC commands, the rest takes care of itself."

When he dropped by to see me after I'd left the seminary, he said, "I told you many are called, few are chosen. It's hell on earth, you know, to be chosen. You've got an interesting life ahead of you, you should photograph it and send me some of the pictures. I'll give you a good 35mm camera and a telephoto lens." He never did.

FIFTEEN

History and Hysteria

Three or four times a summer throughout my seminary years, Father Kitchen used to come by my mother's house and talk me into spending the afternoon with him on my day off from the department store. That was always Monday, and Monday was the day of the week he disappeared from whichever small-town parish he was serving and drove into Regina and made his rounds. "Making the rounds" meant seeing all the people he needed to see and those he thought needed to see him. One of the first stops was the rectory attached to a parish on the wrong side of the tracks in a poor part of town. The priest there was the closest thing Kitchen had to a friend among the Regina clergy, and their friendship had a lot to do with the three or four bottles of duty-free booze Kitchen brought along as a gift every time he dropped in. Kitchen routinely visited the United States by infrequently patrolled routes. He viewed the smuggling of tobacco and alcohol, not as a crime but as the sort of game a Jewish fisherman might have played with Roman authorities two thousand years ago. Kitchen was not a drinker. He was teetotal and almost Victorian in his umbrage against alcoholism, but he had a fondness for Irish priests with a capacity for getting drunk for the sheer joy and hospitality of it. For one thing, it loosened lips, and in his cups (as he would be by the time Kitchen came back to have supper with him), his sodden friend would give him all the libellous and slanderous gossip he needed to fight another round in his unceasing battle against "Archy" — the archbishop — whom he regarded as arch-enemy and arch demon, in league with the legion of demons who had been made bishops on the advice of those who surrounded Pope Pius XII and insulated him from the world. Kitchen was openly and virulently homophobic. He revered Pius XII and was certain that the pope was a man untroubled by lust for men or women; somehow, though, he'd allowed himself to be surrounded by a gaggle of queer cardinals ("Look at their girly wrists, for godsakes," he'd say, thrusting a blunt finger at *Life*). All the appointments to bishoprics during Pius XII's "pontificate of pansies" had been to "members of the club" — "boyfriends of boyfriends." What made Kitchen's point of view less scandalous than fascinating to me was his conviction that Archy and his confederates were altogether too Irish and too repressed to ever actually touch one another. That's what made them so peculiarly dreadful: they were themselves homophobic. He cursed them many times over. It was diabolical for men to lust after men. It was even more satanic for men not to lust after women.

Women needed to be wanted by men. Kitchen revelled in the company of women. He loved teasing women about their need for men and thanked them with backhanded compliments, Quixotic chivalry, and extreme chauvinism. A few women befriended him and many more were perplexed. Making the rounds also meant dropping in on some of "the wives" — he used double entendres whenever he could — and giving them half-crates of eggs or hams or some of the other farm produce that cash-strapped parishioners gave him when they had nothing to put in the collection plate. Or he'd come to town bearing wild meat — duck, partridge, bear, venison. Kitchen was a hunter, in and out of season.

One Monday afternoon in one of my summers away from St. Pius

X, he dropped by our house with some shirts that needed buttons sewn back on. He often came by in the hope that Mom would mend something for him. He was very bad at taking care of himself, crumpled as an unmade bed, tattered, and forever in need of repair. While waiting for my mother to work her magic with needle and thread, he showed me his latest toy, a superscope — the most powerful telescopic sight then on the market — for his Remington hunting rifle. He was attempting to make a marksman of me. I wasn't very interested. When we got in the car, he handed me the scope, and I busied myself looking at things through it. Before I knew where we were, we were out of town and driving in an unfamiliar direction; none of "the wives" I'd met lived out that way. We drove a long distance into the country and down unpaved roads until we neared the farm he said we'd come to visit. He stopped the car and had me blow up a red balloon he took from his pocket. It was just a kid's party balloon, but he wanted it blown up to the size of a man's head. I puffed while he found a bit of string. We tied it to a boundary post and then drove up to the yard and parked by the kitchen door. A woman appeared at the screen but didn't open it. Kitchen bounded out, and I followed him up the steps of the back porch. The woman spoke to him through the closed screen. It was difficult to make out what she was saying because she was holding a wet towel to the side of her face. It didn't cover her blackened eye. Her husband, she said, was up at the barn.

Kitchen sent me back to his car for the scope and his rifle. When I got up to the barn, I could tell that the farmer wasn't pleased by our company. Kitchen didn't seem to notice. He was full of talk about the wonders of his new telescopic sight. He just had to demonstrate it. There and then. He took the gun from me and made a big production of fitting the scope to it. He offered it to the farmer to take a shot at the balloon we'd left up at the road. He aimed and shot. "Missed," he said.

If he hadn't said, I wouldn't have known. The balloon was well beyond normal vision.

The farmer shot again and missed. And a third time.

Kitchen offered me the gun. I declined.

He put it to his own shoulder casually and squeezed off a quick shot and then handed the gun carelessly back to the farmer. The farmer looked through the scope. "You got it," he said.

"Treat a gun like you'd treat a lady. You handle her gently and admire her qualities and smile at her peculiarities, and she'll do whatever you want her to do. If you push her around and make her go against her nature, she'll fight back and hurt you both. A gun like this can kill you," Kitchen said.

On the way back to the city, Kitchen asked, "Why didn't you shoot when I offered you the gun?"

"I knew I'd miss. I'll never be a sharpshooter."

"So what, you're still in the seminary, and you'll never be a priest."

"Why won't I?"

"You'll find a lady or she'll find you first. Don't worry about it. It's better to marry than to burn. Or be buggered."

"I want to meet the author of *A Blue Boy in a Black Dress* before I die," he said. "You must come and drink with me tomorrow afternoon. I live in your neighbourhood."

Those were the first words I heard after I'd said "Hello" into the telephone, before the speaker said his name or enquired after mine. Absolute confidence. I must be the person he wanted. I must do as he asked. Well, I couldn't. Not the next day. Nor the day after. It had to wait till Thursday.

"No later," he said. "I could go anytime."

He wasn't being funny. He had cancer and it was advanced. He kept himself going with a continuous flow of cigarettes and alcohol.

"Just another kind of chemotherapy," he said, "and I get to keep my hair."

He asked me if I'd drink what he was drinking. It looked lethal. I said I'd be happy with bottled water.

He brought me a goblet that sparkled. It was heavy crystal. Family glassware. Engraved. With a crest. The contents had a subtle, wonderful hint of champagne.

"Noblesse oblige," he said. "From California."

It was an extremely hot August afternoon, and the walk to his building had drained me. I was halfway through a second goblet before it hit me that I was being refreshed by an exquisite sparkling white wine with high alcohol content. Not grape-flavoured designer water. Definitely not.

His upper-floor apartment had a sweeping view of the river, antique European furniture, Persian carpets, the gentlest whir of air conditioning, a sense of Italy, gentility not-quite-yet shabby, and many framed photographs of my host with people I thought I should recognize but couldn't from where I was sitting. He'd been in advertising. Public relations. He'd lived among priests, bishops, cardinals, entertainers.

"I live by the gospels," he said. "I saved my best wine for the last."

His name is one of all too many that my stroke erased. Although I met him only once, I'd thought I'd no more forget who he was than I'd ever forget what he had to say to me. He'd invited me over to tell me what he thought I didn't know or understand well enough about the Catholic church.

"You must never forget — it's historical and hysterical. Both. Hysterical and historical."

He'd learned the art of the pause from Jack Benny.

"The church is Roman. Its patron saint is Virgil. St. Peter is just window dressing — like our Polish Pope."

It was pointless to insist that I'd left the church entirely, was an ex-Catholic, could not connect in any way with the current Pope. He would have none of it.

"You know too much about it," he said, "for the church to ever leave you."

I didn't argue the point. He was obviously ill and short of breath. He spoke in little more than a whisper, but there were things he wanted me to hear. I sat back, drank, and listened, because I was the audience he wanted that afternoon. He wanted to talk about Virgil and the Vatican and his childhood in Rome. He wanted to talk about homosexuality and the church.

I took it all in, with too much of his fine wine. This is what I remember.

The church is historical. The church claims descent from Peter and through Peter to Jesus and through Jesus to Adam. What is really the case, and so well established by the Vatican that it never has to be spelled out in so many words, is that the church is actually St. Paul's, and Paul is one of Rome's own — the "Saul" business in Acts is also window-dressing. Paul, Roman in his soul, knows precisely what must be given to Caesar, and he makes Christians pay up like Romans. Never, ever forget that the Vatican reads everything in the Bible through the filter of Paul's letter to the Romans and not the gospels — except Luke's Roman one. The Vatican is Rome and Rome is what Virgil made of it. Inside the Vatican, Virgil is St. Virgil, the prophet who is greater than any prophet in the Hebrew Bible because he hears the voice of God amid the clamour of gods and foresees the changes from pagan to Christian, from political to cosmic empire, without any help from Abraham, Moses, Isaiah, and the others. Virgil sees Augustus as the forerunner to Constantine that Providence prepares. Rome, not Jerusalem, is the city uniquely favoured by God and destined to universal, cosmic rule forever and ever, amen. *Urbs* and *orbis* are one. Virgil is both the poet of Rome and a Christian soul by nature.

As Virgil's *Aeneid* traces the evolution of Rome out of the fragments of Troy, the epic poem blends history with hysteria. Gods no longer simply guide the actions of men through space and time towards a sacred city; their power struggle for control of the divine and the natural threatens to return the world to the chaos from which it emerged. The underworld and the heavens battle for mastery of men's bodies and souls. Right at the beginning, in book one, the queen of the air rebels against the lord of the celestial fires, Juno against Jupiter. It's as hysterical as *Paradise Lost.* History is crucially archetypal. The sword is the cross. The cross cuts both ways. The church is hysterical and historical until swords become ploughshares.

What happens to people who see themselves as both instruments of Providence in the Divine Plan and pawns in the games of Chaos? What happened to him? His personal history was providential and chaotic, he said. Historical and hysterical. He had been an eyewitness to history and hysteria at the Vatican, with Fascists and Nazis outside the gates during the Mussolini and Hitler years, and the Allied advance and liberation. His family, highly placed political exiles in Rome, found asylum within the Vatican for the duration. He was a child, with the freedom of the palaces and squares. Pius XII was immobilized by hysteria, his own and that of his courtiers. The greatest sins of that pontificate were the deeds left undone, the actions not taken, the lives not saved. While Jesus wept, Vatican cardinals and courtiers acquired new paintings from Jewish collectors before German officers could requisition them, redecorated their apartments with bargain-priced antiques from Jewish dealers, dined and drank extravagantly as fiddlers played and boy sopranos sang.

I wanted to know what he thought of the Vatican's actions after the war: sheltering war criminals and finding them safe passages to South America.

He wasn't done with hysteria. Not yet. Hysteria is a displacement of the womb, metaphorical, not physical: from a mother's body to a son's mind. He liked the fact that psychologists had renamed it "conversion disorder." Hysteria was a man trying to be his own mother and making a mess of it. He was riffing now, letting ideas tumble out. The church was hysterical whenever it converted sexual energy into ecclesiology. Holy Mother Church was historically fictitious, hysterically funny. And sad. Tragic. How can any mother look at her son and deny her own sexuality? Or his? Mothers always know both what they are and what they are not, and they're not virgins. The only sexual identity the church openly recognizes in its clergy is the suppression of sexual identity through celibacy. The church has always known that there were homosexuals in the ranks of its priests but has always taken pains never to acknowledge them as such. What a mother! It insists, before the fact, that the majority of priests throughout history have lived celibate and holy lives. Sex enters the official portrait of priests as hysteria, disorder, narcissism.

Thinking of Kitchen's outrageous claims about a "pontificate of pansies," I asked my host if he thought there were many practising homosexuals in the Vatican during the reign of Pius XII. It wasn't an idle question. I thought he might have an unusually well-informed opinion on the theory that some of the highly placed clerics who assisted fleeing Nazis were blackmailed into such activities by accounts of their sexual practices that had found their way into Gestapo dossiers. The Nazis, after all, had made it their business to know everybody's secrets.

Practising homosexuals! How he hated that term. As if it were a profession — practising dentists, practising gynecologists. Or a sport. Practising tennis. Practising golf. Thinking of hitting a few balls, are we? He assured me that the active homosexual priests and bishops he had met were adepts, needed no practice. But he did not want to "out" anybody because he might end up "outing everybody." All the straightest of the straight followed Luther out of the Roman Church. The same thing had happened again in our lifetime, except that straight priests were pushed out by Paul VI.

How had I known that I had a vocation, he wanted to know; what had really led me to the seminary? He told me I hadn't written nearly enough about the way I'd been recruited. Wasn't it true that first as a child in a strict Catholic home, then as a student at parochial school, then again in the altar boy society and the choir, and, most of all, in conversations with parish priests and the Jesuits at my high school, I'd been taught not only to pray every day but to include in my prayers a special prayer for a sign of a vocation to the priesthood? What sign was I told to look for as a signal that Jesus wanted me among His fishermen?

He told me that the signs he was told to look for in his own life became sexually charged when he entered adolescence. He was told to look at the things that separated him from his friends and put him increasingly in the company of priests. He wanted to fuck but he didn't want to make babies. He didn't want to be anybody's father. Or any woman's husband. He was often overwhelmed with the sensation that his own soul was more of a battleground between forces of good and evil than those of his friends and classmates. And these were counted as signs of a vocation by his confessors.

I told him it wasn't very different for me.

Did I understand how boys who had "inappropriate feelings" towards other boys might think it was all part of a strange religious test, and that a passing grade was only to be found in the celibacy of the priestly life? Renouncing sex made the denial of one's own true sexual nature easier to bear and even heroic. He'd tried to be very heroic and failed. Hysterically. He said that flawed logic can't contain our sexual feelings, and some part of us always has to break down or we'll be broken beyond repair in our entirety. He hadn't been broken. He'd come close. That's what he liked best about my *Blue Boy* — I hadn't been afraid to say how close I'd come to an edge that he recognized.

We started talking about priests we'd known who had bailed out of the priesthood during the reign of Paul VI and married almost immediately, sometimes repeatedly. Pope Paul's strict edicts against any form of birth control that actually worked chased heterosexual priests who were sympathetic to women out of the confessional, out of the church, and into marriage beds. There was far less reason for homosexual clergy to leave and many more reasons for them to stay; after all, the Catholic priesthood was the largest men's club in the world.

I told him that when I was in the seminary I'd asked both "inverted" and straight seminarians to estimate the proportion of homosexuals inside the seminary and in their home dioceses. Most answers ranged between fifteen and twenty-five per cent. These days, from what I'd been able to find out, seminarians in North America casually and consistently estimated the proportion of homosexuals among themselves at between forty and fifty per cent, and they think the same percentage applies among the younger priests in their dioceses. I told him a joke I'd found on the Internet: the safest place for a good Catholic to have a heart attack in Denver on a Saturday night was Tracks, a gay bar, because he'd be sure of getting the last rites on the spot.

My host reminded me that he was a Latin by birth, a Roman by upbringing. Mediterranean peoples looked on homosexuality in a different way than North Americans. You were not homosexual if you did it to others, only if it was done to you and you accepted it willingly. Would keeping this distinction in mind halve the numbers, or would doing away with it double the numbers? He repeated that he did not want to "out" anybody. Or everybody. Coming out of the closet was very difficult when the closet was as big as the Catholic Church.

I wasn't asking him to supply gossip. I really wanted to know if he thought people who suppressed their own sexual identity were likelier to collaborate in suppressing evidence of sex crimes and protecting perpetrators from prosecution. Homosexuality among priests and bishops has to be considered in greater detail, I said, both because it was a criminal activity in many jurisdictions well past the middle of the twentieth century and because it is still treated with such opprobrium by so many inside the Catholic community.

He told me why he had not become a priest. He could not convince himself that his sexual feelings were bad or evil. He had tried to do so, and it never worked. Through his failures, he'd learned that keeping those feelings secret led too easily to acts that were evil and corrupt; he didn't offer specifics. What he said was that a person could be a true celibate only after he admitted to himself and others what, precisely, he was denying himself. A person who never did that remained a sexual adolescent. Adolescents in all eras act out sex in inappropriate ways. Adults let teenagers get away with enough of it to get it out of their systems and move on, mature.

The aura of death gave this man a wonderful sense of maturity. He'd suffered worse indignities than his final illness, and they had made him wise and loving. He did not say this. I saw it in his eyes. He asked me to kiss him. On the lips. And I did. He said, "Remember — the church is always hysterical and historical."

I never saw him again.

SIXTEEN

You Can Call Me Al

Shortly after my stroke, one of the team of specialists treating me said, "If you do the work, your body will begin to feel like your own again within six months. It'll take up to a year to feel your mind is your own, but if all goes well, you'll have your own life back at the end of two years." My own life, my own mind, my own body. He stressed that they would be my own but not my *old* selves. Fine, I thought, and started doing the work right away. The first step was to do everything I could to avoid injuring my head further, and that meant keeping my blood pressure down and avoiding any accidental injuries to my head. I only went places where I could go door-to-door by taxi and get past the second floor by elevator. I went back to teaching in less than a month but entered and left the college during off-peak hours, when the narrow corridors of what was once a convent were mostly empty. My office adjoins the classroom I always use, so I didn't have to brush shoulders with masses of students at any time. I was also dependent on a heavy-duty walking stick that kept most people at a comfortable distance. Because the architecture and interior decoration of church buildings from the first half of the twentieth century doesn't vary a lot and I'd toured the building before my college renovated it, I often find its rooms and corridors bring back vagrant memories of Campion and St. Paul's. I couldn't stop thinking how very different this all was from my days at Campion College. At my high school, students owned little of their bodies, less of their minds, and almost nothing of their lives when teachers were around. We were their prey and bullied as they saw fit. They fitted their thumbs and forefingers to the lobes of our ears, their fists to our shoulders, their flattened hands to the backs of our heads, their knees to our butts, their feet to our shins. They did not do all of these things individually to all of us. They were specialists. Boyle was the master of the ear pull, Granville of the sudden whack, LePine of the finger stab in the ribs, Toth of the upper body blow, and Maurice of the kick to the shins. They did not do these things all the time: they were Jesuits and had mastered the first rule of all terrorists — keep your victim off-balance at all times by patting, petting, pushing, shoving, and pummelling in random sequences. They did not do all of this to all of us: they were Jesuits and had advanced training in psychological persecution and spiritual torment. They talked as they walked among us, and told us, in loud voices and, to maximize our humiliation, in such open spaces as stairways, club rooms, and the passageway to the gymnasium, just what stupid slugs we were, and, worse, how much they thought our eternal salvation was at risk. They'd say things like, "I pray for you daily, mister, because I think your eternal salvation is in jeopardy." Our only hope, they told us, was to think as they taught us to think and live exactly as they told us to live.

By August 2003, I'd finished my work with a physiotherapist and was a month into three-a-week workouts with a personal trainer, beginning to do the full range of exercises I'd been accustomed to doing for years. I was working with very light weights, and my stamina was much reduced, but I could look at the wall of mirrors and see myself, rather than just a sick-looking guy with a bad leg, staring back. I still wasn't able to read nearly as much as I wanted or understand what I read as well as I used to but I was reading the *Gazette* and the *Globe and Mail* every morning and looking out at the wider world that I didn't feel I could venture very far into with my damaged body. Travel plans didn't extend beyond Balconville. On an afternoon in mid-month that was as hot and sticky as the one I'd spent drinking champagne and discussing homosexuality in the church with my host a few years earlier, I drank lemonade at home alone in the kitchen and thought about the spiritual bullying Fred Henry, the Roman Catholic Bishop of Calgary, had recently set in motion. Bishop Henry had said that Prime Minister Jean Chretien, a Catholic, could burn in hell for allowing same-sex marriages. Bishop Henry elaborated his remarks at a press conference by saying words with an all-too-familiar ring: "I pray for the Prime Minister because I think his eternal salvation is in jeopardy." He told CBC Newsworld he was unrepentant about his strong condemnation of the Liberal same-sex marriage bill, "[There] is a sense of build-up on behalf of Catholic people who have been saying, 'Bishop, when is someone going to say something to our Catholic politicians with respect to their responsibilities?' The whole process was accelerated by the release of the Vatican of these considerations of the obligations and duties of Catholic politicians with respect to same-sex marriage legislation." The Archbishop of Toronto, Cardinal Aloysius Ambrozic, then sent a letter to his two hundred and twenty-three congregations. It is "imperative," he said, that priests speak out from the pulpit against same-sex marriage legislation and advise Catholics and, in particular, Catholic politicians around the world to oppose such laws. Cardinal Ambrozic ordered the following message inserted into the bulletins at all the Toronto parishes:

> Marriage is a union between a man and a woman. They can, and usually do, conceive and bear children, whom they have the joy and responsibility of nurturing and educating to adulthood. All persons deserve respect in accord with their human dignity. Trying to rename other kinds of

relationships to call them "marriage," however, is inac-
curate.

A lot of people had a lot to say in response to the bishop and the
cardinal. Monsignor Peter Schonenbach, general secretary of the
Canadian Conference of Catholic Bishops, said Henry and Ambrozic
weren't participants in a nationwide campaign; "Every bishop is an
independent entity. It will play out in different ways." Kevin Simpson,
the president of Dignity Canada, a group for gay and lesbian Catholics,
said Bishop Henry "over-stepped the bounds" and invited a backlash
from ordinary Catholics. "What is surprising is that in this day and age
the church thinks it can control the voting patterns of the faithful. Are
politicians who voted to allow artificial birth control doomed to hell as
well?"

In his weekly "Letter from the Editor," Edward Greenspan had
noted in the August 9 edition of the *Globe and Mail* that his paper had
received around three hundred letters on the subject of same-sex
unions in the preceding week and been inundated with submissions for
the *Globe*'s Comment pages. These, he said, "have come from all over
the country and been all over the map," and that the "common de-
nominator is that most of them are brimming with emotion. Rarely
have our letters editors seen an issue expose as many raw nerves." One
of the more notable letters to appear in the *Globe* came from the play-
wright and novelist Tomson Highway:

> For people like us who come from distant, isolated, nor-
> thern communities such as Canada's Indian reserves, it
> seems like only yesterday that we were told by the Catholic
> Church not to marry Protestants.
>
> Why? Because Protestants were evil; because they talked
> to the devil. The ruling not only created much human misery,
> and drove rifts within communities that were, and are to

this day, irreparable, it destroyed families. And you don't even want to know what they said to us about Jews and Muslims.

Are you going to let "them" do it again? Are you going to let "them" do even more damage? Are you going to let "them" create even more human misery, more rifts, more hatred?

The *Globe* became a useful servant of the thinking public in that August 9 issue by running Michael Valpy's analysis, "Why Same-sex Marriage Became a Sin." Valpy, who knows his history, pointed out just how fudged the Christian church's "proprietary claim" to marriage and its definition really is. He pointed out, quite rightly, that no priest is ever recorded officiating at a wedding in the Bible, that biblical law presents marriage as a commercial transaction in which a wife is purchased, that nothing in the Bible prescribes monogamy or proscribes polygamy, and that it contradicts itself on the subject of divorce. The definition of marriage most of us have grown up with comes from the legal *Digesta* of the Roman emperor Justinian (483-565): "Marriage is a union of a man and a woman, and a communion of the whole of life." Valpy noted as well that it wasn't until the Council of Trent (1545-1563) that the Roman Catholic Church formally declared marriage to be a sacrament and required that marriages between Catholics be celebrated in a Catholic church, that the Church of England took another two hundred years to issue the same order, and that it took until the eighteenth century for marriage to be formalized as a religious event in all countries of Europe and, for the most part, in the Americas.

In a letter printed in Montreal's *La Presse* and widely quoted by the *Globe* and other English media at the same time, Father Raymond Gravel, a priest in the parish of Saint-Joachim-de-la Plaine and chaplain for the Laval police force, said the Vatican's position against same-sex marriage is "discriminatory, hurtful and offensive . . . for everyone who

works to promote human rights and to re-establish justice and equality."
He attacked the church's hierarchy as outmoded and sick, saying that
we're all more in need of "words of hope rather than a verdict of condemnation." Addressing the Vatican's censure of rape victims in Bosnia
who were getting abortions, Father Gravel asked, "How can this church
still speak in the name of God?" Father Gravel added that his church is
wrong to teach that homosexuality is deviance. "Everyone knows that
sexual deviations are not exclusively related to gays, but to everyone
who has to live his or her sexuality clandestinely. In this matter, the
clergy has become masterful, as numerous priests frequent parks,
saunas and public washrooms to let off steam. . . . For the church, the
only way to live one's sexuality is within marriage in a bid to have
children. It's time to rethink that vision. Sexuality is not only about
having children, it's about showing love and tenderness. We are all
sexual beings."

So we are. The wonder of it is that we pay any attention whatsoever
to those who still attach unequivocal shame to our sexual natures and
believe and disseminate the view that a brute, animal urge must be
hurtful, violent, and eminently suppressible whenever it doesn't serve
willy-nilly to reproduce our species. There's a way out of the current
impasses between church and state on the issue of same-sex unions,
but it's doubtful if these particular bishops and their pope are willing to
do the reasonable thing. Law and morality are not co-extensive. To
legalize something does not make it moral. The commandment "Thou
shalt not steal" may make theft immoral, but thefts of all sorts are legal.
In a sane society with a sober justice system, actions are not made
crimes unless they unreasonably interfere with the liberties of others.
Even for those who regard same-sex relations as inherently immoral,
there's no inconsistency in tolerating homosexuality while outlawing
pedophilia. What happens if civil unions are allowed to take place
between any two adults who fully consent to what they're doing and
don't interfere unreasonably with the liberties of the rest of us? Not

much of anything. The principal threat to family life remains what it has always been — the physical abuse of women and children by the dominant male of the household. Not one of my fellow seminarians ever told me of being sexually abused by a priest in childhood — pedophilia is rare — but an alarming number were only too willing to share the dirty little secret of their upbringing, the gross physical abuse they suffered at their fathers' hands. Some of those who talked about it inside St. Paul's walls admitted that they were so frightened of harming women and children in turn that a celibate, unmarried life appealed to them greatly. This was not true of those like me, whose fathers may have raised voices in anger but never hands to strike their wives or children.

The sort of questions that need to be asked are the kind I was taught to ask by the Basilians at St. Thomas More who taught me philosophy before I went on to study theology and canon law. Prime Minister Paul Martin took his own BA in philosophy with the Basilians at St. Michael's in Toronto in the same era. Will he be able to bring the sides closer together through reasonable discussion? It's not impossible, but such discussions demand recognition of what Father Gravel gets and bishops Henry and Ambrozic miss. The four decades that now separate us from Vatican II have witnessed an enormous growth in human knowledge and its dissemination. We now know much more about how everything — our bodies, our minds, our environments, our global opportunistic diseases, our politics, our weather — actually works, and we know that almost everything is infinitely harder to understand than we thought it would be. We are no longer small groups of illiterate, stateless people living off the land, surviving by our wits, depending on what women and donkeys can carry, listening to seers delivering divine messages from out of the whirling visions that engulf them and passing them off as eternal truths, and condemning everyone who doesn't believe as they do. Well, at least, most of us aren't quite so tribal.

* * *

"Bond? Is that really you?"

"How did you recognize me?"

"Not the beard. Or beret. Definitely not the jeans. You've moved down market, but who hasn't? Nice coat, though. Your laugh. Nobody else laughs like you. Which paintings are you looking at? What are you interested in? I used to own that one. And that one beside it. My lawyer said he'd take my pictures when I couldn't come up with cash to cover his fees. He and my ex-wife are still wondering what happened to them."

In November 1994, my beret, beard, and completely un-Bondish *savoir faire* seemed to alarm a phalanx of security guards every time I used the elevator in my hotel in Toronto. They were overseeing an auction of important Canadian paintings, and their nervousness made me unable to resist going into the showrooms and seeing for myself what treasures they were so zealously protecting. I listened to the ladies who shop at Hazelton Lanes do their impersonations of fine art criticism and laughed. I looked at the paintings and laughed again.

And Al recognized me. Actually, I'd already spotted him but hadn't made a move in his direction. I didn't want to embarrass him. In our days together at St. Paul's seminary, he'd been choir-boy innocent, easily embarrassed. His looks had coarsened but hadn't suffered a lot of alteration, and there was still pink in his cheeks. In a neat grey suit, white shirt, black tie, Al looked like somebody's chauffeur. He said he was self-employed, sort of, since the limo outside belonged to his former brother-in-law, and driving it would provide rent money only until life improved and he was back on Bay Street. Wherever. He had time for a drink. We went into a very dark bar. Diet Coca-Cola for him. A beer for me.

"It wasn't just your laugh that gave you away. I saw your picture in the *Globe and Mail* last year. I looked you up in the library. I even read that first book of yours, the one you did with the other guy, Mike Mason. I liked his novella better than yours."

"A lot of people did. Some critics thought he was going to be at least as well known as Guy Vanderhaeghe. I still get asked 'Whatever happened to Mike Mason?'"

"If I still drank, I'd bet you the price of a liquid lunch I could answer that one. It impresses my new girlfriend that I know a guy who knows Mike Mason. He's one of her favourite devotional writers. She's given me *The Mystery of Marriage* to read."

"And have you read it?"

"No. The relationship is working okay right now. I don't know that I want to think about marriage again, not yet. I'm still burned out from my last one."

"Maybe you should read Mike's new book, *The Gospel According to Job*."

"I don't know if I want to think too much about my losses either. My ex-wife took the kids, the house, the car, our savings. She got it all. Cocaine did bad things to my judgement. I did bad things to her and the kids. She has custody. If her brother didn't like me more than he likes her, I wouldn't have work. What did your divorce cost you?"

"I'm not divorced."

"Sorry, I didn't know you were gay."

"I'm not that either."

"You didn't get married?"

"I'm married. I got married and stayed married."

"You must be about the only one of us who did. I have three kids. How many do you have?"

"None."

"Are you trying to live like a monk?"

"No, not at all. Not even like a bohemian."

"So you don't live off your writing like Mike Mason does?"

"His books sell in the tens of thousands. I teach."

"You were smarter than me, Bond. You got out of the God business while there were still teaching jobs to be found. Then again, it was probably harder for you to leave. When I got out, everybody was leaving. Every teaching job I went after, there were ten ex-priests and twenty ex-nuns applying. That was '76. They all had doctorates and loads of experience. I didn't have any experience, not even seminary teaching. I had an MA in pastoral psychology. I'd been a marriage counsellor."

"Why didn't you stay with that after you left?"

"It was too demoralizing. I seemed to pull more marriages apart than I put back together. That probably wasn't such a bad thing. A lot of those people were stifled in their relationships. But at the time, it didn't feel right. "O, the damage done." Neil Young. Do you listen to Neil Young? You were such a Dylan freak! My girlfriend is a lot younger than me. She listens to Neil Young. Nirvana. There was a lady at the last marriage encounter session I ran as a priest who was more interested in seducing me than getting things straightened out with her husband. We both liked Haydn symphonies. She left him, I left the priesthood, and we came east to Toronto. It felt really good at the time."

"And now?"

"I brought too much baggage to the relationship. I was more smothering than her husband. That was her story. Mine is that it cranked her engine to screw a priest. As soon as I stopped being a priest, the oil went out of her crankcase. I've always had less trouble with cars than with women."

"And she took the kids and left you broke?"

"No. Not her. She and I didn't get married. She went back to her husband. No, somebody else caught me on the rebound. My ex-wife turned me into an automotive leasing consultant and a family man. Oil and vinegar. I got too slick. Slid out of control. I have a lot of regrets about that one."

"What about the priesthood? Do you have regrets about leaving it?"

"I couldn't have stayed. I wanted my stomach to stop hurting, and I wanted to be kissed passionately by a woman."

"Is that all there was to it?"

"If that sounds pat, it's just because I've said it a few times. It isn't a line, but it's a hook to hang a line on. I used to tell women, *I'm still very hungry*. Food or sex, they could take their pick. What about you, why did you leave?"

"I lost my faith."

"Did you find it again?"

"No, not what you'd call faith."

"So you don't go to church?"

"Not unless somebody dies. What about you?"

"I stopped being a Catholic when they elected John Paul II. He just doesn't get it, does he? He just can't see that there's any reason for intelligent people to resent the Vatican's hypocrisy. Maybe if he'd had to face the problems of raising kids on two inadequate incomes, maybe he'd understand birth control and divorce better. What does a guy who can hand out money by the millions to back Solidarity in Poland know about the problems of people raising families? What does he know about women? You do know what I'm talking about."

"Why did you really leave the priesthood?"

"Are you going to use this conversation in the book you said you're writing?"

"I may do. Do you mind?"

"No. But could you be economical with the truth?"

"How?"

"Could you make me out doing better than I am? And change my name, too. And I wouldn't mind you mixing me up a little with the other guy we've been talking about."

"What about calling you Al? What about a nice grey business suit? What about having an affair with somebody else's ex-lover and letting you drive your brother-in-law's airport limousine?"

"Yeah, that's nice. By the time people read it, it could even be true. He appreciates the way I keep it nice and clean. I'm clean. I haven't taken a drink or drugs in over a year. I've got a lot of people praying for me. When I was a priest, we had the Spirit and then we lost it, and the Spirit left us and went elsewhere. I'm waiting its return. I'm glad you don't hold to your old faith. The Spirit is talking to you. It's no accident we met today. Come and pray with us tonight."

"Where do you do your praying these days?"

"The Airport Vineyard. My brother-in-law got me interested. You've heard of it?"

Indeed I had.

Ever since Pastor Randy Clark arrived from Saint Louis, Missouri, to hold his first prayer meeting on January 20, 1994, at the Airport Vineyard, a storefront church in a strip mall in the industrial belt near Pearson International, a Spirit revival had gripped Toronto and drawn tens of thousands to, as the participants say, "do carpet time, soak, get drunk in the Spirit and catch the Fire." Apologists for the laughing, weeping, jerking, leaping, collapsing, Lion-of-Judah-roaring, soul-searching, rocking-and-rolling, slain-in-the-Spirit participants told us that all of this joyful noise was divinely ordained confirmation of a prophecy uttered by Marc Dupont, a Vineyard staffer: Toronto is to become the New Jerusalem, a place of miracles and wonders from which spiritual blessings will spread like wildfire to the four corners of the earth before the Second Coming of Christ. They called it "the Toronto Blessing." I suppose they still do. In 2003, it isn't making headlines the way it used to, but a friend visited it recently and says it's still doing what it does to build the City of God among us.

When I was growing up in Regina, some of the people in my neighbourhood believed they were living in God's Promised Land. I don't mean Tommy Douglas and the CCF Party, who clearly understood that the New Jerusalem had to be built by blood, sweat, and tearing down capitalism. I mean the people of the Latter Rain Movement. This religious phenomenon erupted among a small group of Christians in North Battleford in 1948, spread throughout the province, and had large repercussions elsewhere. Followers of the Latter Rain credited their leaders with the power to work miracles in the name of Christ by the laying on of hands. What separated these people from many other faith-healing groups was their interpretation of healing as a sign of the power given by the Spirit to the healer to discern the inner lives of those they touched and to prophesy their fates in terms that weren't entirely benevolent. The services I attended as a teenager convinced me that this curious blend of self-help and self-loathing was emotional fascism of a very high order. I was readier to convert to Karl Marx's claim that religion is the opiate of the masses. That's when I stopped going places simply because a girl said she liked me. That's when I started attending meetings of the Labour Progressive Party on my own. In 1994, I really didn't want to see firsthand what hold this offspring of the Latter Rain had on Al, so I opted instead to give the rest of Toronto a much closer once-over than I had in a while and see for myself if I could find any other signs of Jerusalem the Golden within it.

But a decade ago, after having spent even a short time with Al, Toronto seemed to me to be more like a three-tiered purgatory than a twelve-gated city. Talking to friends and strangers in shops and bars and on the street, I sensed escalating unrest, increasing repression, a heavier police presence, more racism, less community activism, a greater tightness in the throat about immigration. Toronto seemed more Chicago-in-the-making than Jerusalem-on-the-Humber.

Then again, what do I know of Jerusalem? I've not yet made it as far as the Promised Land. I have travelled further in my head on the wings of a well-upholstered sofa than ever by car, bus, train, boat, or airplane; the greatest of my adventures have been induced by books — reading many, writing a few. When I think of the New Jerusalem, and that doesn't happen often, it tends to take on the proportions and qualities of the British Museum's old Reading Room. I like libraries. I like books, not as objects but for the life they contain. When I'm not in the company of writers such as Barbara Gowdy, Brian Fawcett, or Catherine Bush, who are as smart as their books and every bit as civil, the happiest times on my visits to Toronto are spent in bookshops. That's where I find the fuel necessary to challenge and out-think the optimistic idea that constantly threatens to overtake the realist in me, the one that suggests the future is simply the present with more options.

SEVENTEEN

Catching Fire

I don't go looking for those I once knew in seminaries. Some came looking for me in the first decade after I left St. Paul's, either to meet for a drink and rehash old times or to see if I could help them get a teaching job. I bumped into enough ex-seminarians and ex-priests in that way or at airports, conferences, and on street corners to believe that Al's life isn't typical. As far as I know, none of my former classmates died in Vietnam. If anybody has gone to jail, I haven't heard of it. Quite a few have been treated extensively for depression. A lot married within a year of getting out, some to ex-nuns, others to widows who had small children. Those for whom marriage didn't work and some others now lead single lives of eccentric intellectual interests and minimal emotional attachments. I don't have much evidence one way or another, but I suspect that the majority are leading fairly ordinary lives. Except at night. When aging bladders wake us, I suppose many lie awake for a long time, thinking ourselves failures because we never lived up to the expectation thrust upon us by the priests of our childhood: we would become great warriors in the battle for the souls of men.

Al was always out of the mainstream. Among the Holy Joes, the saintly seminarians in Ottawa, there was a small group somebody had nicknamed the Bleeders because of their devotion to the Sacred Heart of Jesus. They were reputed to hold nakedly emotional prayer meetings in a secret location. Al had been rumoured to be a member. They'd been security-conscious and I'd been uninterested: I was into meditation and chanting in the chapel. At the beginning of 1967, during the weeks before my walk to the river, the Bleeders got very animated. Word reached them in the basement storage room, or wherever it was they met, and filtered up through the seminary pipeline of supernatural events in the United States: the Spirit had descended upon some Catholics in a new and wonderful way. I was long gone from the seminary before Charismatic Renewal became public knowledge.

What happened is this. In January 1967, three non-ordained members of the theology faculty at Duquesne University in Pittsburgh felt themselves filled with the same gifts of the Holy Spirit that were part of the early Church, the gifts St. Paul writes about in a cautionary way in I Corinthians before extolling the glories of love: healing, miracles, prophecy, discernment of spirits, speaking in tongues, interpretation of tongues. The Duquesne theologians started prayer meetings among Catholics that spread to East Lansing and Ann Arbor and across the continent to San Francisco. The leaders interpreted this outpouring of the Spirit among them as God's answer to John XXIII's prayer that Vatican II might set the Spirit free in the church. They saw themselves doing what the bishops had failed to do: bringing blessings directly to the people. This vision gave them enormous energy and ambition. Convinced that the movement was meant for the whole world, Stephen Clark, Ralph Martin, and Gerry Rauch acted boldly. Together with Jim Cavnor from Ann Arbor, they held leadership conferences and developed training programs and initiated publication of educational materials. Within five years, the Catholic Charismatic Renewal Movement recruited over a hundred thousand members and spread into two dozen other countries. It was so successful that it had a major impact on the charismatic movements among Protestants, which had started several years earlier, inspired largely by the Latter Rain Movement. No small part of the popularity of Charismatic Renewal came from the fact that it emerged from universities. Previously, the Spirit had shown a distinct preference for the less well-educated.

After serious in-fighting, senior clergy in most mainline Christian denominations accepted charismatics grudgingly. On principle, they couldn't be rejected out of hand, since I Corinthians doesn't question the availability of such gifts among ordinary Christians. However, church authorities were hard pressed to maintain equanimity in the face of some of the alleged miracles and wonders. The curia tamed and trained the renewal movement by organizing it parish by parish and placing it under the control of priests appointed by the local bishop. Inevitably, many of those who'd felt the Spirit moving in their hearts were more comfortable doing their praying well away from the precautions of established churches, in places where they met less opposition when they did the things they really liked to do, such as organizing their own Masses in each other's kitchens attired in beads, sandals, and flowing homespun shirts and skirts. Homemade multi-grain bread, pretty good French wines, lengthy kisses, and protracted embraces while some sang, others played guitars, a few danced and everybody murmured or moaned such slogans as "Jesus is coming." From 1972 onwards, individual Christians seeking prayer fellowship caused a dramatic growth in nondenominational assemblies, some of which make extensive use of mass media, most of which are connected with networks of pastors who don't restrict local autonomy, and all of which regard the various outpourings of the Spirit as normal.

Toronto's Airport Vineyard is one of several hundred churches linked together in a fellowship begun by Carol and John Wimber in California in 1976. The Vineyard sees itself as a Third Wave, continuous with but distinct from earlier movements. Because of its lack of a Catholic connection, its openness to fundamentalism, and its down-home easy-listening soft rock style, the Vineyard has been called "countrypolitan Christianity." Toronto's Airport Vineyard is its Azusa Street.

Azusa Street?

In 1906, at a series of momentous meetings in a storefront church on Azuza Street in Los Angeles, William Joseph Seymour felt the Spirit descend upon him. Just four days before the San Francisco earthquake of April 18, he started preaching that the world was being shaken by the Lord and would catch fire. His followers took this as a sign of the Final Days, a period some of them believe will last precisely one hundred years from that day forward. Seymour was the son of slaves, but his new movement crossed racial barriers. It spread west to India and looped back east to Chicago before re-converting Britain and establishing beachheads in Canada, Hong Kong, and Korea. It called itself Pentecostalism, but it didn't exactly descend from the heavens.

In the mid-nineteenth century, dissenters in the Methodist church had developed the Holiness movement. Basing themselves on St. Peter's prophecy in the Acts of the Apostles that a kingdom of God will be established on earth in which the wicked will be punished and the just rewarded, Holiness taught that the Holy Spirit empowers good works — healing and miracles. Holiness disciples worshipped with passionate prayers, vigorous songs, and personal testimonies that induced the ecstatic loss of muscle control: rocking on the heels and rolling on the floor, jerking, twisting, and shouting. These actions got them dismissed from other churches and known in the popular press as Holy Rollers. In 1901, Charles Fox Parham, a pastor from Topeka, Kansas, stitched various Holiness groups together into the Pentecostal faith and elaborated its practices and doctrines. Seymour desegregated Parham's movement, gave women a larger place within it, and brought worldwide attention to it.

For Seymour and Parham and their many Pentecostal descendants, Christian doctrines are not fixed and frozen in the words of the Bible for literal interpretation; the living word of the Spirit comes first and is witnessed by personal testimonies in front of the congregation. Doctrine is guided, developed, and shaped by the power of the Spirit, which moves people to preach and tell stories. The Spirit brings freedom, and freedom means a limited hierarchy and high levels of lay participation. The movement divided into many denominations, some along segregationist lines, but all Pentecostalists insist that baptism is by the Spirit, and the sign of the Spirit is the ability to speak in tongues.

Speaking in tongues or glossolalia is frequently misunderstood. It's neither exclusively Christian nor merely gibberish. You can find it in the New Testament but also in Patanjali's *Yoga Sutras* and in the *dhikrs* of some orders of Sufism. It's not pathological, although it is out of the ordinary. Its sound units aren't words; they don't convey meaning. To speak in tongues is not to speak an unknown language. It's a spontaneous, wordless singing of phrases of equal length, each of which is accented on the first syllable in a consonant-vowel, consonant-vowel sequence with rhythmic throbbing and haunting intonation. Just about anybody with musical ability can learn to do it, and doing it involves an alternation of two different arousals of the nervous system. People say its after-effects are like post-coitus but more extensive. Glossolalia makes a person feel good all over and more loving towards more and more people. Although Pentecostals would use different language to say so, they understand that religion is above all the uniquely human process by which individuals are persuaded non-rationally to subordinate their self-interests to the interests of the group. Anything that fails to do this is not "of God"; they may not be able to say precisely why the world works this way and not another, but they know that it is so.

Whatever else it does, Pentecostalism totally reshaped American musical tastes within its first two generations. This isn't its only accomplishment, but it's the one most people know at least a little about. Pentecostal music is heartfelt, enthusiastic, subjective in expression, emotional in style, loud, and electric. Pentecostals sing, shout, clap hands, leap, dance, and march to Jericho with trumpets, drums, steel and electric guitars, and Hammond B3 organs. Pentecostals put a spell and a spin on gospel music, and quartets such as the Blackwood Brothers reached out and touched musicians from Memphis to Nashville and on to Harlem with propulsive music featuring double lead high voices, novel harmonies, and escalating rhythms that insisted upon improvisational gifts. Beyond music, Pentecostalism's foremost appeal is its personal connection with God through the Spirit, its absolute certitude, its literal belief in prophecies, the eradication of addictions to tobacco, alcohol, drugs, sex, and gambling. It began a worldwide transformation of Christianity in the twentieth century that's more profoundly life-altering than the Reformation because it makes the personal the final arbiter of the political: retool yourself and make society rethink its conventions to fit you as snugly and smoothly as the sort of bespoke suit from Saville Row that male members of the Royal family favour.

All of this was not only predictable, it was predicted. Not prophesied, predicted. Not by a Bible-thumper, but by a dandified cartoonist and essayist in a custom-tailored three-piece suit with a double-breasted waistcoat — Tom Wolfe. Wolfe's celebrated essay "The Me Decade and the Third Great Awakening," published in *Mauve Gloves & Madmen, Clutter & Vine* in 1976, did something more than just take the social pulse of the moment. Wolfe saw that the Me Decade of the mid-sixties to mid-seventies and its aftermath had actually begun with the economic boom that followed America's wartime spending. Wolfe asserted that the boom's trickle-down effect brought prosperity to every class of society to an extent never before seen in history. Wolfe slowed his rhetoric long enough to grudgingly exempt slum dwellers from this miracle of capitalism, but he still noted in more or less the same breath that Californians on welfare had incomes greater than newspaper columnists in Britain or factory foremen in Italy. For Wolfe, general prosperity meant, among other things, the breakdown of conventional society as individuals chose to create new lives entirely of their own design. For Wolfe, such people were the first Americans outside the plutocracy to use their wealth to reconstruct their own selves. Millions arrived at the previously esoteric truth that a spark of God within every human soul can be united with other sparks in a new ordering of the universe, a new righteousness that can express itself as sexual swinging, selfhood seminars, theosophy, fundamentalism, or Pentecostalism.

By and large, readers of Wolfe followed the lead of the media and picked up on the sexual swinging and the selfhood seminars, the glamorous stuff he satirized. In a rush to read the personal advertisements to find out who was just how willing to do what to whom, they overlooked the larger, more serious point Wolfe was making: every major religious wave that developed in the West has started out in just this same way with a flood of largely secular ecstatic experience. The other matters might be more sensational, but the religious issues — supernaturalism, fundamentalism, and Pentecostalism — needed the most careful examination. They formed the leading edge of a wave that's changing the American way of life more radically than the revolution that followed the preaching of Jonathan Edwards or the westward migrations after Joseph Smith communed with the angel Moroni. The crest, Wolfe predicted, will challenge our notions of serial immortality (that is, living so as to create a better world for our children) and usher in the greatest age of individualism the world has ever seen.

Nearly thirty years later, it's clear that Wolfe read the signs of the times very well indeed. Pentecostalism and its charismatic offshoots are spreading faster and wider than any other faith in North America or the rest of the world. They've gained somewhere around half a billion very enthusiastic followers in less than a century and will double to a billion by 2050. Within a few years, one in three Christians is likely to be Pentecostal or belong to some other charismatic community, and be very vocal. Given that its everyday North American converts are drawn mostly from the active membership lists of mainline churches, the religion of such enthusiasts is profoundly influencing the general landscape of Christianity down the street and across the world. If Pentecostalism fails to become the dominant form of Christian belief and practice, its failure will be caused by internal paranoia and racism or by its own downplaying of personal experience in favour of Biblical fundamentalism. But I don't think it will falter. Pentecostalism and its offshoots will grow because they claim to teach immutable virtues, not temporal values, and a lot of people still see a need for all the character, courage, truthfulness, trustworthiness, respect, responsibility, and fairness they can find within themselves in the face of mounting social and political chaos. Most of all, Spirit-centred Christianity offers its adherents an uninhibited source of joy. What it doesn't provide is social cachet. It's so very much the religion of the moved and shaken and so little the religion of the movers and shakers that its advance has scarcely been noticed by the mainstream media.

Ultimately, the shape of Christianity to come always depends, not on some alleged breath of God but on the kinds of all-too-real cruelty that prevail in the world and the degrees of moral panic they precipitate. Christianity has always been reactive; it improvises responses to events beyond its control; it isn't self-contained, an independent entity which the world affects only by broadening or narrowing the scope of religious freedom. Although the Catholic Church does not understand itself as a reflection of fluctuating social currents, historical investigations simply do not support the contention of its adherents that it is a timeless supra-cultural presence in the world. Ferocious debates and alternative traditions about Jesus and his death erupted among the first gatherings of disciples after his crucifixion, and ever since those first rounds of theological debate, the winners have constantly de-monized their most intimate enemies. From this process of demonizing the enemy came both the scapegoating of Second Temple Judaism in the gospels and the *ressentiment* of the Revelation of John, a fearsome apocalyptic construction of social disillusionment with Roman im-perialism.

Assuming that humanity does not have to face up to the realities of either great nuclear catastrophes nor massive environmental calamities, and that the international political community has some success in controlling warlords, gangsters, and zealots in Eastern Europe and the Middle East, the dominant form of Christianity that is now coming into its own is going to be shaped by forces beyond the pope's or any other European's control and beyond American military interven-tionism. For the first time since the seventh century, the majority of Christians are not of European origin. Within another generation, Christianity will be firmly centred in equatorial climes; it will be massively Spanish, Portuguese, and English speaking. The transition from a European cultural base to an equatorial one is inevitable. At the moment, equatorial Christianity is very young, unstable, diverse, and poor, but its presence and pressure are undeniable. In Africa, where it is powerfully allied to Catholic rituals and pageantry and takes fire from charismatics, it's more than matching Islam in growth and moral fervour. African Catholics are pressuring the curia to allow priests to marry to legitimize the children they are already fathering. The Vatican will relent after the death of this pope or that of his successor. A married priesthood is less than a generation away. The unacceptable alternative is that Catholics in Africa will be split off from Rome by a preacher with the power of Luther who will forge a new alliance with Latin America's Catholics. In Asia, Christians are likely to sever religious ties to the West, which they may demonize in ways that we have not yet seen. In China, Christianity is likelier to break free of male domination sooner and faster than elsewhere in the world; leadership will rest on women who heal, exorcise, and teach a personal morality that combines dignity and discipline. That's what leading analysts predict, and I've seen no counterclaim that's equally convincing. It's the height of presumption and folly to even hazard a guess as to what consolations may be found in the gospels by women whose sense of the future bears little relationship to our patriarchal European past.

When I wrote of this new Christianity in *A Blue Boy in a Black Dress*, even some of my closest friends thought I was enamoured with it. Actually, I'm only fascinated, not enthralled by it. I am just acutely aware of its power in shaping what Philip Jenkins, the author of *The Next Christendom*, and others have taken to calling "global Christianity." The Eurocentric Christianity we see dying all around us still attracts the attention of newspaper editors; fuelled by the For Sale sign on the Trappist monastery at Oka, the *Montreal Gazette* spent the summer of 2003 preoccupied by the dying off of monasticism in Quebec. Pentecostalism and its offshoots rarely draw equivalent media attention. The largest, fastest-growing, most dynamic centres of Pentecostal and charismatic Christianity are such places as Kinshasa, Buenos Aires, Addis Ababa, and Manila. Nigeria, Kenya, Ethiopia, Mexico, Brazil, and the Philippines are now the world's leading Christian countries. What is happening there is far more important in religious terms than what any pope continues to think, do, and urge. Africa and Latin America will soon account for fifty percent of all Christians in the world and an even higher percentage of active ones. Anyone who wishes to be a serious student of Christianity as it exists now needs to know far more about Africa than can be found in even the best university libraries.

The level of knowledge about Africa's actual religious life is so low among North American savants that far too many have accepted and far too few have challenged the claim that "In the long run, Muhammad wins out." Samuel P. Huntington, the leading tactician of the Bush administration's global strategy, makes this assertion in *The Clash of Civilizations and the Remaking of the World Order.* But Islam will not be the world's largest religion by 2020, as Huntington insists; Christianity will maintain its 3:2 numerical dominance for the foreseeable future. Huntington's assertion that "Christianity spreads primarily by conversion, Islam by conversion and reproduction" is equally fatuous, as Philip Jenkins amply demonstrates. But Huntington is often quoted and Jenkins is ignored. According to Jenkins, the new Christianity as synthesized in Africa and Latin America does not conform to the liberal, activist, revolutionary model propagated by theologians such as Canada's own Gregory Baum. "The dominant current in emerging world Christianity is traditionalist, orthodox, and supernatural," Jenkins writes, and then he gives each of those terms a spin that puts them at considerable distance from what Pope John Paul II and the Vatican mean by them.

Emergent Christianity reads the Bible in ways that makes itself look like something wholly different from the faith in which I was raised and divergent from even the charismatic eruptions around me in Saskatchewan in my childhood. Like North American Pentecostalism, it's at home and comfortable with dreams, prophecies, miracles, good works, hospitality, and rigorous moral behaviour. Where it veers away from any Westerner's ability to plot its future course is in the sense of oppression, exile, and martyrdom it shares with the earliest Christian communities. Jesus not only talks to African, Latin American, and Asian Christians about exorcism and healing; He tells them what to do when on trial for their faith, how to respond when expelled and condemned by families, villages, competing religious authorities, and evil secular rulers. In equatorial and southern climes, Christians live in constant danger of persecution and forced conversion. Torture, torment, suffering, death, and hoped-for resurrection are daily realities in Guatemala, Rwanda, Indonesia, the Sudan. Half the world's exiles are in Africa, and millions of them are Christians. Exile and return are for them precisely what the Bible makes them out to be — the rise and fall of Babylon. The Revelation of John is their prophecy, their truth, their epic, their reality, the confirmation of their profound pessimism about what they can expect from the rest of us.

EIGHTEEN

City of Churches

The room in which I sit to do much of my thinking and all of my writing is on the mid-slope of a small mountain on an island near the north shore of a mighty river flowing through a great hardwood forest. It's easy to forget that the island, the mountain, the river and the forest exist because I'm in the densely populated, thickly concreted west end of Montreal, a city connected to the north, south, and west shorelines of the St. Lawrence River by many bridges and a couple of tunnels. The shores are cluttered with buildings, the river is slowed with refuse, and the forest is hiding itself in the face of urban sprawl and acid rain. Some local historians say that Côte St-Antoine, the upper border of the city block on which I live, follows the path of an ancient Indian trail that began in the Iroquois village of Hochelaga. All that's actually on record about Hochelaga is that on October 3, 1535, Jacques Cartier and his men read the gospel to the natives of Hochelaga and climbed Mont Royal to survey the surrounding country. The Indian village was far from navigable water and surrounded by fields of corn. A triple row of palisades encircled about fifty bark-covered longhouses. By the time other explorers reached the area, nothing remained of that village. We don't even know who its inhabitants were. After Cartier's departure, these people disappear from history, leaving behind words in an otherwise unknown language collected by the French from prisoners captured further downriver.

When Cartier read the gospel to the natives, he read it to them in Latin. In Europe, the Reformation was in full flower. A year earlier, Henry VIII asserted control over the English church. A year later, Thomas Cromwell began dissolving the monasteries. Ten years later, the Council of Trent reasserted Catholic hegemony and instituted the Roman Mass throughout its territories. It would be another four hundred and thirty years before Vatican II would allow the use of French, English, Mohawk, and all other vernaculars in its services.

Introibo ad altare Dei.

Ad Deum qui laetificat iuventutem meum.

If happiness is a reliable indicator of joy, I didn't discover much joy in the religion of my childhood except in serving as an altar boy. In catechism classes and confessionals, I learned too young about the sins the priests and nuns called pride, arrogance, disobedience. I had to discover for myself, much later and too fearfully, the blessing of self-confidence, of being true to whatever it is that is actually me, by following the dictates of conscience. I learned too young to keep my tears hidden and my anger banked and to feel my way forward down on my knees, my nose pressed against a mesh screen, speaking my deepest fears into a closet so dark that it swallowed the church that enclosed it. I can still feel the priest's breath, smell the talcum, sense the quivering ear hairs of a man who offers words of kind advice that always promise a peace of mind that never arrives. That condemnation of anything and everything that set me apart from others made me very discontented, dissatisfied with everything about me as a person, forever wanting to be elsewhere, inside somebody else's skin, among great rivers, wild trees, and high mountains.

There are no rivers or mountains around Regina, and the only tree native to the place and not planted, so local legend had it, was the large willow in whose branches I rested on my hikes across a seemingly unremarkable prairie landscape to the nearest point of interest — the Regina airport, and my daydreams of flying away. Nothing I really wanted ever seemed accessible. My true place in the world was somewhere else, far away. Some in my family claim that the eyes of my childhood were always set south to the Wild West of the Dakotas and Montana. I did spend an inordinate amount of my early life wearing a cowboy hat, six-shooter and holster, chaps, spurs, a sheriff's badge, and cowboy boots. Part of me wanted to be a very bad guy, a gunslinger, an American. But black-hat, fast-draw, Billy-the-Kid fantasies formed the smaller part of my childhood, as small as playing games with children my own age, as small as school, as small as the city of Regina. The place that most filled my imagination and answered my longings when I stood within the cool vastness of the Regina Flying Club's hangar and watched Trans Canada Airlines DC3s arrive from Winnipeg was to the east. It was to the east of Winnipeg, beyond the east of Toronto, Montreal, the Maritimes, and even England.

There are people who claim that Catholics did not know the Bible — at least not then, not in the fifties. But I knew the Bible. I had enough of it to know that my true home was on the Jordan River beneath Mount Zion, in a land where olive trees grew, and I was startled and discomfited to be a child growing up in Saskatchewan. It seemed very wrong to be so distant from God's own country, and I knew of only one secure way of getting there, the Catholic way. I followed the prompting of priests at Mass in an automatic and unreflective Latin while I read the English text of scripture passages in my own prayer book given to me by my father. Later, I read Knox's Oxford English translation of the New Testament, which Father Walt gave me when my father died, until

I worked up the courage to commit the serious sin of studying the King James Bible in the Regina Public Library without obtaining the permission of any priest. I worked at being more grown up than my Catholic world easily allowed, dreamed of the Promised Land, and lived constantly in a state of anxiety about the present state of things and my own miserable life. It was no way to live, but it was the best way of life I knew.

There's a public park at the very top of Westmount's little mountain. A road rings it. From the park, I can look out over all points of the compass. Because I can look all ways, none draws me more than another. Since coming to Montreal, I've lost most of my restlessness. Since my stroke, I'm more rooted here than ever. Overlooking this city on a very clear day in late summer 2003, certain inescapable conclusions about religion in our time drew in on me. This mountain is much lower than the mountain from which Nietzsche sent Zarathustra forth into the world to speak of the death of God and the will to power. The will to power gripped Pope John Paul II mightily. In the spring of 1995, while I was writing *A Blue Boy in a Black Dress,* he launched *Evangelium vitae,* his gospel of life, his eleventh encyclical in seventeen years. Women are an easy target for men who do not know them intimately through marriage, and how Pope John Paul II targeted them, how Pope John Paul II rushed to judge them (and those men who would stand by them) and assert their right to control their own bodies. This pope wrote that people like me are sliding towards totalitarianism by insisting on the permissibility of contraception and abortion. John Paul II could neither see nor hear Nietzsche's madman rushing through the city below his own hilltop, carrying a lantern at noon, crying out, "God is dead. We have murdered him." The God whose death was announced is a strictly European cultural entity, the enthroned monarch of "God Save the Queen," the protecting bulwark of "A Mighty Fortress Is Our God," the God in whom America trusts on its currency, the God who is on both sides in all the wars Europeans and North Americans have waged

against themselves but always on our side in wars against the rest of the
world, the God of athletes who is there when every point is scored in
every cup and bowl game, the star-struck God who shows up at the
Oscars and Grammies. That God is dead. His history is written. His
houses lie beneath me in the hundreds, and they are virtually empty, and
they will not fill up again.

Montreal was once called the City of Churches, but a diminishing
number remain in service for the few who attend. Some buildings fall
each year to the wrecker's ball, and more are recycled to other purposes.
The major ones — St. Joseph's Oratory, the Anglican and Catholic
cathedrals, Notre Dame Basilica, and the key downtown markers of the
Scots Presbyterians and the English Methodists who once ruled this
country from their estates in the Golden Mile — will remain as places
for marriages, funerals, seasonal concerts at Christmas and Easter,
stops on bus tours for visitors from elsewhere, and centres for outreach
programs to the homeless and others who aren't helped in the ways in
which they need day-to-day help by hospitals and social agencies. On
any given Sunday, excluding Easter, it's been estimated that somewhat
fewer than two million Canadians attend church. That means that
nowadays there are about the same number in the pews nationwide as
there were Catholics at Sunday Masses in the greater Montreal region
fifty years ago. It's a pretty safe bet that many European-style churches
will change allegiances and welcome Equatorial Christianity's refugees
and house forms of worship and give voice to theologies beyond easy
comprehension.

Over sixty per cent of contemporary churchgoers now belong to
so-called evangelical Protestant, Baptist, Reformed, Pentecostal, and
more loosely affiliated prayer fellowships. In my neighbourhood, the
largest mainline Protestant building passed into the hands of Seventh
Day Adventists a few years ago. The other churches that are thriving
extend an evangelical welcome and a helping hand to a broader and
broader spectrum of new Canadians from the southern hemisphere. St.

Stephen's Anglican church, which was built in 1903 to serve the ultra-fashionable Montrealers who first established residences in Westmount, dwindled to a handful of aging families and went up for sale in 1990. Then, suddenly and spectacularly, it revived into a parish of five hundred young people by dumping Anglican traditions for the songs, signs, and spiritual manifestations of the Vineyard Ministry while nominally remaining within the Anglican communion. Not long afterwards, the building began to fall apart, and the new congregation had to relocate.

Religions come, religions go but religion in some form or another is always with us. Religion is one of the near-universals of social behaviour. During the sixty millennia separating us from the earliest decorated grave, humanity has produced on the order of one hundred thousand religions. Stating that religion is found in nearly all times in nearly all societies is not to imply, as some intellectuals continued to say as late as the first half of the twentieth century, that all religions are more or less the same. No, they're not. They aren't all pluralist philosophies tending to pure monotheism, as some idealists had it. If that were the case, Unitarianism would have supplanted all other churches, synagogues, mosques, and votive altars by now. Nor are religions irremediable clots of superstition, as some materialists insisted. If that were the case, religion would disappear as science advances. The fact is that growth in scientific understanding and technological complexity seems to generate stronger and more diverse religious responses. This is not a uniform phenomenon. Unbelief has risen, but it is much more localized, clustered among the most and the least technologically advantaged in the industrialized world. It seems that we progress by knowledge but continue to draw inspiration from the very beliefs our knowledge invalidates. We are Adam and Eve, eternally returning to Eden to eat the fruit of the tree of knowledge that will make us like the gods, who then expel us so that we can return once again. As Nietzsche said in *The Genealogy of Morals,* mankind would rather have the void as purpose than be void of purpose.

By Pentecostal reckoning, the falling-down laughing, crying, shouting, roaring ecstasies so prevalent at the Airport Vineyard and its relatives are questionable religious experiences. These behaviours can be learned. They can be easily faked. They can be the devil's doing; religious ecstasy is merely physiological until it is certified as spiritual and holy by upright, outstanding behaviour and confirmed by speaking in tongues. Speaking in tongues is the only certain gift of the Holy Spirit, and Pentecostals say it's temporary, the one true sign of hope amid the troubles of our times that the second coming of Christ is imminent. The Pentecostals I've met are, on the whole, balanced believers, with a lofty view of the Bible as Revelation but also deep reverence for personal religious experiences and a conspicuous passion for building communities that are cross-cultural and transnational. Like less charismatic but equally evangelical fellow Christians, they give generously of themselves and their resources to the larger community. They feed the homeless, provide clothing and shelter to the indigent, nurse the sick, and comfort the afflicted. They do have the annoying habit of expressing themselves in a Bible-based language that is so determinedly naive and unpoetic as to appear ridiculous when it isn't simply impenetrable to outsiders such as myself. Pentecostals fascinate me because they seem to provide more intimations than many other groups about how greater peace might be achieved in the twenty-first century than prevailed in the twentieth. Peace cannot be imposed by military power nor willed into being by good-hearted people; it has to be built little by little out of cross-binding loyalties. Pentecostalism and its offshoots make it difficult for people to regard each other as discrete entities on the basis of racial, linguistic, national, religious, ideological, and economic interests. They offer a kind of socialism that is a lot less doctrinaire than what I find elsewhere, and they are much more successful at charming capitalists into doing the right things.

If Pentecostalism were simply a fervent expression of hope that humanity can only find peace and spread it by building societies that are neither driven nor riven by racism, fascism, greed, or panic, I'd wish all its followers well and say no more. What I object to in it, what I object to even more forcefully in the Airport Vineyard and its ilk, and what I found totally unconscionable in the Solar Temple is probably their only common bond. They create and celebrate hysteria, based on the assertion that a new, improved world is beckoning us just around the corner, and all we have to do to find it is break rapturously free of this one. To say this is simply to dull the mind without touching any emotional centres deeper than fear and the urge to flee. Members of the Solar Temple took the coming of a new world so seriously that one or some of them stabbed an infant through the heart and inserted a wooden stake in his chest because their leader believed this innocent was the Antichrist. When I heard that, I felt wounded again in the place that religion had once occupied in my own heart. The Solar Templars' cold-blooded attitude to life, their fiction that a comet was about to bring a new, improved world silenced something in me, stifled the impulse I've had since childhood to create fictions of my own.

To make up a story, I must find a place to begin, and the feeling grew in me throughout most of the past decade that there are no more beginnings for the West, that the life I lead and the lives I know best are trapped in an end-game. The only characters I can come up with look at the world like children caught outdoors in Nietzsche's twilight. Seventy million men, women, and children were killed by warfare, starvation, deportation, political murder, and disease between August 1914 and the "ethnic cleansing" of the Balkans. The horror is that this slaughter arose, not from barbarians at the gates, but from National Socialism, Fascism, and Stalinism emerging from within the high places of our own civilization. Refined intellectuals, artistic virtuosos, scientific eminences all collaborated actively with these totalitarian demands or, at best, remained indifferent to the surrounding cruelties. All this damage done to humanity as a species since 1914 makes it difficult for me to grasp the co-existence in time and space of Western super-fluity with the starvation, destitution, and infant mortality which now afflict some three-fifths of humanity and conceive of effective ways to correct it. That certainly seemed to be the view of any characters I invented, even those whose thoughts didn't go back even further to add on the genocide of another sixty million or more brought about by the slave trade and the empire-building of the eighteenth and nineteenth centuries. Those stories don't need to be told again, my characters said, they've been recorded. But when I asked my phantasms to give me a plot from which I could spin a tale they wanted, they lost all words, made animal noises and gestures, and died in more and more grotesque ways. I don't think they were urging me to start writing horror fiction. They seemed to be telling me that they were devolving into less and less human states because the magnitude of waste is so extravagant and deadly that evolution may reverse. This same thought pressed in on me every time I picked up Alexander Solzhenitsyn's *The Gulag Archipelago* and tried to come to terms with what actually happened to those relatives of mine and their neighbours who didn't escape to the West.

The possibility of human devolution means, among other things, that the nature of creativity has been utterly and irredeemably altered. The old storyline that runs from Genesis through Revelation, the one about paradises being lost and regained, seems more and more used up — jargon, hype, and propaganda erode and undermine solid relation-ships between words and reality. The rationale and credibility of any future that is not already part of our past has become questionable. How can anyone respond creatively to that? All was collapsing inward — the stories I could write had already been written. Feeling this way, critical not creative, for most of the past decade I kept my attention focused on the details of my everyday experiences and tried to remain as reasonable as possible in the face of fear and regret, danger and hardship. These seemed to be the only things that could save me from the all-consuming madness that I saw around me. Being reasonable meant simply accepting more and more diversity and embracing it in all its messiness, keeping my mood as liberal as I could. In practical terms, it meant reading as much as I could in all the areas where my reading might make a difference to the people I live and work among. Whatever else I was, I was a reader of books, and I gave myself over to reading even more than I had as a child on Angus Crescent in Regina more than half a century ago. Among all the books I read, many were about Jesus.

I was done with the Catholicism of my father, I was done with any and all forms of Christianity, but I was not done with Jesus. My first year in the seminary wasn't just a roller-coaster ride; I was as thrilled as a child rising upwards on a ferris wheel when Dr. B. told us seminarians on the eve of our Christmas holidays in 1962 that the gospel writers had prefaced the teachings and death of Jesus with pious fictions — the Nativity story was a mythological hook created in Rome to pull in passersby and amaze and convert them by a miraculous and senti-mental birth in a strange part of the world. There was no manger, no stable, no birth in Bethlehem for Yeshua of Notzereh *aka* Jesus Christ. Jesus did exist. He also died because the Romans wanted him dead: he challenged people to think for themselves rather than surrender passively to authority. His death was not the end of him. His words, his acts, his effect on others, and his life have been written about ever since.

NINETEEN

Testament

Books about Jesus outnumber those about Shakespeare, Napoleon, Lincoln, or Hitler. There are at least two dozen diverse and sometimes wildly fanciful novels about Jesus and ten dozen biographies readily available in English or English translation. This is a modern phenomenon. St. Paul, arguably the first Christian, discounted the importance of needing to know much about Jesus when he wrote in II Corinthians 5:16, "Even though we once knew Christ in a human way, we no longer think of him in that way." Only a few facts about Jesus were essential to Paul and his followers. Paul simply will not have it said that Jesus was born of a virgin; such a superstition was incompatible with seeing him as Son of the Lord God. It's anything but revolutionary to say that Jesus is not divine by virtue of a miraculous birth; that idea goes straight back to Paul. The gospels of Matthew, Mark, Luke, and John provide only a few highly selective "facts" but many powerful sayings attributed to Jesus within bare-bone narratives that serve mainly as vehicles for a proclamation of Jesus as Christ and Christ as the key to the Kingdom of God. That's what has always counted most for most Christian believers. But not all. There have always been believers who wanted to fill in the large empty spaces left in the life of Jesus by the official accounts or discover the things he said that remain unrecorded. And there have always been sceptics, inside and outside the church, who have questioned the credulity of those who believe that Jesus did and said what the gospels say of him — in part because these accounts disagree with one another about so many "facts." The early church accepted the writings of Matthew, Mark, Luke, and John despite their diversity and forcefully rejected the attempts by Tatian in the second century to reduce the four to a single "gospel harmony." At the same time, the church dismissed or lost a welter of other lives of Jesus. An ancient legend holds that each of the original apostles (including Judas in some accounts and Mary Magdalen in others) created gospels of their own. The Gospel of Thomas and the fragments of others that have been found subsequently are, on the whole, bizarre and reveal little. This is also true of the many local legends about Jesus that flourished throughout the Middle Ages and still provide fodder for modern writers: Jesus travelling throughout India, Jesus settling down to married life in the south of France with Mary Magdalen and raising a family whose sons fathered a royal bloodline in France.

In 1846, a then unknown English writer who called herself George Eliot translated the German philosopher David Frederick Strauss's *Life of Jesus* into English. Strauss attempted to explain why even highly educated Christians believed in events that did not have any historical basis, were contrary to common sense, and violated the natural order. Using the resurrection as his key example, Strauss concluded that religion is an expression of the human mind's ability to generate myths and interpret them as truths revealed by God. He characterized Christianity as a stage in the evolution of pantheism. His book, a *cause célèbre*, fostered a new focus on Christ's life as a mythical construct that neither supernaturalist believers nor rationalist doubters could adequately interpret or ever understand. Charles Dickens reacted to Eliot's translation of Strauss by reaffirming his own comfortably orthodox beliefs and writing the thoroughly conventional book *The Life of Our Lord* for children. When Ernst Renan, a French historian, published his own *Life of Jesus* in 1863, the debate became more complex. Rejecting Strauss's scepticism about the value of the New Testament as a historical document, Renan read the gospels as carefully as possible and analyzed them in terms of his own travels in Syria and Palestine and against whatever he could discover in the archeological record. For Renan, Jesus was an uneducated but wise Jewish prophet from a green and shady rural Galilee. He inspired a romantic religion of the heart that few parched urbanites in Jerusalem could accept and that many city dwellers throughout the ancient world would misinterpret and corrupt. Renan's Jesus preached that the individual conscience was in direct connection with God and that there was no need whatsoever for any institutional religion. Jesus, in Renan's view, inadvertently provoked both the Jewish priesthood and the Roman empire to such an extent that they retaliated by killing him and pressuring his disciples into making him over into what he never was — a fierce polemicist and a miracle worker.

By the beginning of the twentieth century, academic conflicts and controversies between mythologists and historians over who Jesus actually was and what he might have actually said and done led the great German theologian and Bach scholar Albert Schweitzer to publish *The Quest for the Historical Jesus* in 1906. Concluding that all post-Gospel lives of Jesus say much more about their authors than about their subject, Schweitzer declared the quest to find Jesus in the gospels or anywhere else absolutely futile. He abandoned theology and music, took up medicine, set off for Africa as a medical missionary, and inspired many to follow once again the unhistorical, unmythological Christianity preached by St. Paul. This began the tradition in which novelists imaginatively recreate Jesus in response to their own spiritual crises, a lineage that includes D.H. Lawrence's *The Man Who Died*, Robert Graves's *King Jesus*, Nikos Kazantzakis's *The Last Temptation of Christ*, Jose Saramago's *The Gospel According to Jesus Christ*, and Norman

Mailer's *The Gospel According to the Son,* as well as an assortment of fictions that regard Jesus from unorthodox viewpoints by Morley Callaghan, Anthony Burgess, Guy Davenport, John Updike, Reynolds Price, Jim Crace, Simon Mawer, and, most recently, Nino Ricci, whose *Testament* failed to attract as much attention or stir up as much debate among Canadian readers as I thought it might. It seems that few Canadians wanted to argue about a Jesus who would have been, quite literally, a Roman soldier's bastard if a marriage of convenience hadn't been hastily arranged by the young woman's family.

In his fictional treatment of the life of Christ, Ricci accepts the ancient Talmudic tradition that the father of Jesus was a Roman legate (although he does not name him Pandira or Pantera as the early rabbis did, or follow the lead of those modern writers who want to equate him with the Roman archer Tiberius Julius Abdes Pantera, who was stationed in Palestine until 9 AD). As readers of Ricci's other novels already know, few writers have more sympathy and understanding for those who bear the mark of "illegitimate" birth. *Testament* doesn't merely accept Jesus's irregular parentage as a possibility; it proclaims it early and often, explores it from several vantage points, and makes it a key element in the sequence of events that led to the arrest and crucifixion of Jesus of Nazareth. Ricci's Jesus is also a decidedly human Everyman, riddled by contradictions and internal conflict.

When I interviewed Ricci for a piece I was writing for the *Vancouver Sun,* he told me that he hadn't set out to write a deliberately provocative and inflammatory novel about Jesus. "What I'm trying to do is look at this character — this probably historical personage who has come to us as Jesus — and to try to understand him outside the religious tradition of seeing him as divine and imagine what such a person might have been as a human." The things that most concern Ricci in this ancient tale are the same things that dominate his other books and preoccupy me: estrangement from the dominant society, conflict between generations, family strife, opposing world views, and the search for selfhood.

"What I was not trying to do is to recreate a true historical Jesus, or even, for that matter, to debunk anything. I don't have enough of an investment in Christianity at this point to want to debunk it, but I do have an investment in western culture, and the Christian tradition obviously has influenced everything about western culture. In the twenty-first century, it's hardly a revolutionary statement to say that Jesus is not divine. It's an attempt at understanding." I wondered for a moment if I wasn't hearing an echo of my own voice.

It has taken nearly a century of diligent archeological and textual work by dedicated scholars and the discovery of caches of ancient manuscripts on the shores of the Dead Sea and at Nag Hammadi in Egypt to develop firmer methods for creating more nearly objective lives of Jesus in our time. Over the past twenty-five years, several vigorous works have emerged in North America, among them, John Dominic Crossan's *The Historical Jesus: The Life of a Mediterranean Jewish Peasant,* E.P. Sanders' *Jesus and Judaism* and *The Historical Figure of Jesus,* and John Meier's multi-volume *A Marginal Jew.* What distinguishes these Jesus scholars from their predecessors is that they seek to understand Jesus within the context of Jewish life in the first century and provide a more nuanced view of where Jesus might have fit in. Even so, they each view Jesus in a different way. Crossan sees him as a preacher of radical egalitarianism who offers a way of healing to an impoverished, powerless peasant society. E.P. Sanders shifts the emphasis to the future; he pictures Jesus as a prophet who prepared people for the coming of God's kingdom. John Meier combines present and future, viewing Jesus as a teacher who sees God's kingly rule as already present but not yet complete.

When I asked Nino Ricci about books that influenced him, I was not surprised to hear that he'd read *The Historical Jesus.* "Crossan's book doesn't say that much about Jesus, and in some ways that's what was helpful about it. It says a lot about the social context he comes out of and makes an argument for what Jesus could have drawn from that context — the idea of Jesus having been influenced by Cynic philosophy and so on, which does come up in my novel. I owe a lot to him for establishing that context." Ricci's Jesus — in the novel, Yeshua of Notzereh — is so radical an egalitarian that he treats women in a resolutely modern way, and they respond to him with an extraordinary, myth-shaking naturalness. Viewing Jesus through the eyes of *Testament*'s two Miryams is extraordinary. Mary Magdalene has come down to most of us as a redeemed prostitute, although there's no scriptural evidence for this characterization. Ricci rejects the stereotype and makes Miryam of Migdal less melodramatic, more easily understood as a young woman in search of a future that doesn't free her from being a daughter only to entrap her as somebody's wife. One of the titles traditionally given the Blessed Virgin Mary is Our Lady of Sorrows, and that's the essence of Ricci's Miryam the wife of Yehoceph — a mother who struggles helplessly to comprehend the decidedly different, often difficult, sometimes impenetrable stranger who is always her son but never her husband's child. Ricci, who has achieved the status of feminist because of his equally open sensibility to the minds and hearts of highly vulnerable, uneducated women in his previous novels, told me, "The women's points of view are a natural for me, in that they are certainly missing from the traditional accounts. We never really get to hear from the women, and yet they are there, which is one of the surprising things about the Jesus tradition. The inclusion of women does seem a revolutionary aspect of his ministry."

Much as I liked Ricci's women, I think I liked his cagey and opportunistic Yehudi — Judas — even better. My would-be mentor Father Kitchen knew that other priests called him a son of a bitch and worse. He didn't care; he almost gloried in it. The only thing that really mattered to him was that he never gave anyone reason to call him a "Judas priest" — a compromiser, a seeker after earthly rewards. One of the other bits of advice he gave me was this: "Remember, it wasn't Jews who had a hand in getting Jesus put to death by the Romans. They were *priests* first, Jews — and very bad Jews — second." If there wasn't so much human tragedy involved — so many young lives deprived of all the joys and consolations of normal sexual awakening and quickening — the abuse of children by Catholic priests and their protection from prosecution by bishops would be monumental in its irony in a church whose greatest inspiration should always have been Jesus of Nazareth, the very sort of outcast boy (as Ricci makes wonderfully clear) that cagey abusers and opportunistic predators of the priestly caste are always so willing to sacrifice.

TWENTY

Anger Management

Since my stroke, I have never once asked myself why it happened to me or what could I have done to prevent it. I'm just not built that way: I've known too many real victims of the twentieth century's great horrors to think of myself as victimized in any important way. So I busy myself with doing whatever the doctors say has to be done to keep from bruising my brain a second time — taking taxis and elevators, avoiding crowds and stress, exercising as my physiotherapist and my personal trainer have instructed. Much as I want to, I still can't absorb and retain much more than the barest of facts about the things that a stroke does to a brain and the effects it has on self-identity. I've had three MRI examinations, and I've actually seen images of the original damage and the healing that has taken place. Neurologists have explained what is presently known about the neural pathways that congregate in the portion of the brain that my stroke affected. I know a little but I do not know enough, and reading with the kind of close attention that books about cognition demand is still out of the question. So I look into myself and track what happens, and, as soon as I could follow the plots and keep the characters straight, I started looking at things novelists are good at revealing about self-identity. Mark Haddon's *The*

Curious Incident of the Dog in the Night-time came to me as a gift from my wife in the spring. It's narrated by fifteen-year-old Christopher Boone, who is autistic. Christopher is unable to fathom emotion; the routine, order, and predictability of mathematics, logic, and science shelter him from the mess the rest of us live in. There's a lot Christopher doesn't understand about being human, but he does know humans aren't animals. Unlike a dog, who will chase a cat despite having its broken leg full of metal pins, humans don't forget the pain of their wounds and the miseries of the operating theatre so readily, or fail to foresee the consequences of running on a broken leg, stitches breaking, searing pain. We have pictures on our mental screens of things separated in time and space and level of abstraction from what is in front of our eyes. But those screens can also fool us into thinking that brains are special and totally different from computers: Christopher knows that a lot of people think some kind of little man, a *homunculus,* sits inside the human head looking at the screen, "like Captain Jean-Luc Picard in *Star Trek: The Next Generation,*" and they conclude that this person is their true self. Christopher says, "people always think there is something special about what they can't see, like the dark side of the moon, or the other side of a black hole, or in the dark when they wake up in the night and are scared."

Through Christopher, Haddon shows us that we might all be better off if we were willing to allow ourselves to be a bit autistic — more logical, less emotional, more honest, less willing to suppress the complexity in ourselves and the world simply to get ahead. Christopher doesn't like novels "because they are lies about things which didn't happen and they make me feel shaky and scared." But since my stroke, it's things that do happen that make me feel shaky and scared. I can't yet pick up Steven Pinker's *The Blank Slate: The Modern Denial of Human Nature* and open it to the page I'd been reading on January 27, 2003 — the third page of Chapter Thirteen, "Out of Our Depths" — and grasp the full extent of the mismatch between the purposes for which our cognitive faculties evolved and the purposes to which we put them that Pinker discusses there. It's extraordinarily frustrating because I feel myself in a variable state of mismatch with my environment, and I want to ground my experiences within a conceptual system that gives me a clearer sense of how to operate better with whatever I have available to me. Human reasoning, as Pinker explains it, isn't based on a single general-purpose computer, but on multiple operating systems, and each module, stance, faculty, mental organ, or reasoning engine — the terminology isn't set — is appropriate to only one department of reality. It's easy enough to recite his tentative list of ten such systems: intuitive physics, intuitive natural history, intuitive engineering, intuitive psychology, a sense of space, a sense of number, a sense of probability, intuitive economics, a mental database and logic, and language. It's more difficult for me to explicate the key intuitions at the base of each in ways that leave me confident I understand them. Pinker adds to the others three further components, "for which it is hard to tell where cognition leaves off and emotion begins," and it's really these three I most need to figure out: the system that assesses danger based on fear, the system that assesses contamination based on disgust, and the moral sense. I don't want fear, disgust, or an impaired moral sense getting the better of me, but all I can pull out of Pinker's prose and keep straight is what a predicament all three of them place us in, because understanding in these domains "is likely to be uneven, shallow, and contaminated by primitive intuitions." We remain dependent on "analogies that press an old mental faculty into service, or on jerry-built mental contraptions that wire together bits and pieces of other faculties."

When I try to think about disgust, I keep remembering how contaminated I was at the end of five years in the seminary — the ache in my stomach, the sourness in my breath, and the stink in my guts. I'd swallowed too much too quickly without nearly enough chewing — too many eggs, too much red meat, too much Spam, oceans of milk and coffee, all of it served up by nuns who took the revenge of the table. There was more than this to my bellyache and sourness: a man must work at being a priest to get it right, and I bit down hard and grew tense, burned out my guts with guilt, mortification, and male competitiveness. That made me sicker than the food. I left the seminary ultimately with an enormous appetite to be me, whoever that might turn out to be, in a world that was other than the one I'd believed in until the faith a Catholic world demanded became impossible. Faith is holding on to whatever you can't walk away from, however hard you try to give it up. Having walked to the river, it was easy to take the taxi that took me away from St. Paul's, the trains that took me to Regina and back east to Hamilton. I felt I was doing the right thing and I was unafraid. But I was also very angry, an angrier young man than even angry young men ought to be. My bad temper took years and years to cool down: it was the frustration of a person impaired in his ability to respond constructively to those with authority over him. I was foolishly uncooperative and consistently acted in ways that diminish rather than enhance academic careers. It could have been worse: I could have been self-destructive.

People who seem hell bent on self-destruction through sex, drugs, or God-intoxication don't actively try to harm themselves. Heroin users don't shoot junk into their veins to get criminal records or die in an alley; they get high to feel at peace. In *Straight Life*, Art Pepper, one of the supreme alto saxophone players in jazz and one of its saddest drug users, writes:

> I felt this peace like a kind of warmth. I could feel it start in my stomach. From the whole inside of my body I felt the tranquility. It was so relaxing. It was so gorgeous. . . . I looked in the mirror and I looked like an angel. I looked at my pupils and they were pinpoints; they were tiny, little dots. It was like looking into a whole universe of joy and happiness and contentment.

It's the after-effects that are toxic. The Jesuits who insistently drummed a sense of impurity into me in high school did so in order to help me. They weren't trying deliberately to create an insecure, neurotic, sexually impaired young man. They weren't monsters. I can't make them the butts of the kind of venomous rhetoric and outrageous satire Terry Eagleton engages in. I can't write of any of them what Eagleton writes in *The Gatekeeper* of the headmaster of his school, Brother Damian:

> He ought certainly to have been strangled at birth, or buried alive in infancy in some desolate stretch of bog-land. . . . Damian spent his life in charge of the spiritual development of children, and had about as much human understanding as a tortoise. . . . It was a point of pride with him to discourage sinful individualism by not knowing a single one of his students by name. . . . He was as indifferent to individuals as a lavatory attendant, and regarded his students simply as potential sources of academic glory. . . . In the end, all the world could find to say [in his obituary] was how spotless his clerical collar was. . . . In death as in life, he represented much of the truth of the Roman Catholic Church.

What I can write of the truth of my life is that along the way from my years as a Catholic altar boy and seminarian to where I sit now, I've found that the world in which I'm most at home is the one that comes as a simple gift from the natural order. We're all called upon, more times than we can possibly count in advance, to start anew. A frightening illness, a new job or the loss of an old one, a marriage or a remarriage, a divorce or a death, a birth of one child or the graduation of another — they are all impossible hurdles, and yet they all become mere episodes in the waxing and waning of life among the living. We are ultimately stardust; I prefer the narrative epic of stars and neurons disclosed by science to any of the myths propagated by religions. Science takes in more with greater eagerness and somewhat better techniques of self-correction and asks for no more belief than this: that physical laws are consistent with biological laws and the visible universe is everywhere subject to explanation. To believe this is to remain open to the unknown.

In 1975, Edward O. Wilson published *Sociobiology: The New Synthesis*, a book out of its time. Politically unfashionable and scientifically premature, it provoked enormous controversy among readers who saw in it a theory of biological determinism rather than a prolegomena to a new scientific discipline. The controversy was provocative in another sense as well: it led Wilson to undertake a thorough investigation of classical and contemporary Marxism, and he turned his clarification of the final chapter of *Sociobiology* into *On Human Nature*. The controversy also turned Wilson into a very public and active conservationist.

Edward O. Wilson is a hard man and a hard thinker. Tom Wolfe has dubbed him Darwin II. *Sociobiology* is oversize, unwieldy, six hundred pages of double columns, not a thing to peruse in electronic form if you want to harvest even a little of its greatest yield: a love of biodiversity, what he terms *biophilia* elsewhere. Wilson is a man of his time and place and reads too much of his America back into human nature (as Steven Pinker, one of his intellectual heirs, also does), but he gets biophilia right. Biophilia is the inborn affinity human beings have for other forms of life, an affiliation evoked by pleasure, security, awe, fascination, revulsion. It is a love of otherness. To my way of thinking, it's the closest we come to the God who makes Adam and saves Noah and the furthest we can get from the one who casts Adam and Eve out of the garden and drowns Noah's world.

God may or may not be the beginning and end of everything; the concepts are largely indefinable and the hypotheses are untestable. The complex mental processes that have created and continue to sustain religious beliefs have been wired into our neural apparatus by thousands of generations and ancestors numbering in the millions. That doesn't make them true, but it does make them powerful and habitual. Wilson says that "the enduring paradox of religion is that so much of its substance is demonstrably false, yet it remains a driving force in all societies." Rituals arising from the falsehoods embedded in myths can move us meaningfully from one stage of life to another and help us place ourselves within the world. Such rituals are the seeds for the noblest and most glorious achievements in music and poetry, story and dance, art and architecture.

Like the past, the future is only one of our daily considerations. It's healthier to focus on the present for its own sake. The present is everywhere available in the real world, and when we focus on it, life grows comic because it's the nature of comedy to be inclusive, not dismissive. We're all right as long as we're laughing, and we're laughing as long as we're running our own show; tragedy arises when we surrender too much to those who want to direct us, whose terrible will to power insists that life must be harder than death and that a blurring of the imagined and the real in varying gradations of virtual reality is preferable to the immediately real and realizable.

When I chose death over life, I did so out of a combination of poor judgement and the lack of self-awareness. What looks like irrational behaviour now was perfectly sane to me then because it was motivated by frustrated desires for love, self-esteem, acceptance, success. I didn't understand why my own strategies weren't working, and I resented having even well-intentioned friends explaining my behaviour to me.

But human beings are what we are, and we are part of the nature of things. Our fundamental nature is a welter of genetically resonant adaptations suitable for Ice Age hunter-gatherers that are largely archaic and atrophied in most of our daily circumstances. This isn't all that we are; the choices that have brought us to this point are only a subset of possible choices. To get beyond this point, to see that there are other endings for us than apocalyptic conflagration, we must recognize what Thomas Merton found when he looked in the poems of Chung Tsu:

We have seen a fire of sticks
Burn out. The fire now
Burns in some other place. Where?
Who knows? These brands
Are burned out.

G.K. Chesterton's words in his first novel, *The Napoleon of Notting Hill* (1904), still seem to me the last word on the subject of why darkness continues to exert such power over us:

One of the games to which [the human race] is most attached is called "Keep tomorrow dark," and which is also named . . . "Cheat the prophet." The players listen very carefully and respectfully to all that clever men have to say about what is to happen in the next generation. The players then wait until all the clever men are dead, and bury them nicely. They then go and do something else. That is all. For a race of simple tastes, however, it is great fun.

EPILOGUE

In India, there's an old saying that when one needs a teacher, one finds the teacher one needs. In my four years of high school at Campion College, I needed many teachers; I found only one — Mr. McKay, my grade eleven English teacher. He wasn't a Jesuit. He was a young man, probably only four or five years older than myself, with a recent degree from the University of Saskatchewan. He told us that he was teaching for a couple of years to make enough money to return to university and study law and that he was teaching at Campion because he didn't have a teaching certificate. Mr. McKay did not teach as my other teachers taught, and the lack of formal training might have been the reason. He taught with poetic passion, with a sense that life was all too easily lost. He read us Wilfred Owen and other poets of the Great War, read us T.S. Eliot, introduced us to James Joyce. Or I think he did — I don't know how else I found my way to Joyce's 1907 collection of poems, *Chamber Music*. I bought it not knowing that Joyce claimed the title was suggested by the sound of urine tinkling into a prostitute's chamber pot. Through *Chamber Music*, I found my way into Joyce's fiction — *Dubliners* and *Portrait of the Artist as a Young Man*.

Sometimes now I hear faint reverberations of Mr. McKay's voice in my own as I try to link the sexual experiences of poets, ancient and modern, to those of my students through their common humanity. What I know about teaching, I learned mainly by reaction against those who taught me at their age, Jesuits who decreed that much of what I wanted to read was out of bounds, on the church's Index of Forbidden Books, beyond me, not subject to any discussion even when their subjects were the everyday substance of our lives. In Joyce's *Portrait*, I found a little of myself and a good deal of the religious life of Campion College — the devotions of the Sodality of the Blessed Virgin Mary, the soul-searing retreat.

Stephen Dedalus visits prostitutes nightly and I was a virgin, but mortal sin is mortal sin, and the greater difference between Stephen and myself seemed then to reside in the facts that he had found a sense of peace and quiet in his sins, whereas I found none in mine, and that there was less hypocrisy and guilt in his feelings than in mine. But like him, I too still felt a connection to the image of the Virgin Mary and a sense that She could help me out of my sinful ways. Again, like Stephen, I found it strange that I derived great enjoyment from learning intimately the details of Church doctrine. At my school's retreat, the subjects were the same as at Stephen's — death, judgment, hell, and heaven — and a Redemptorist orator made us fear for our souls with a description of the Day of Judgment that hit us in our softest spots. Hell, in Joyce's novel and Campion College's chapel, was a place crowded, tight, and dark, stinking from all the filth of the world, on fire with a fire worse than any fire on earth because it does not consume its object but preserves it. And hell is exacerbated by all the damned, who struggle against each other, blame each other for leading them into sin, and curse each other. I felt the hot shame of my sins as Stephen does of his and wanted forgiveness as desperately. Stephen goes to a beach to think and suddenly has an epiphany. Contemplating becoming a priest, he sees a beautiful girl standing in the water. As he walks away from her, he realizes that it is not wicked to want what's beautiful in life. I did not have that epiphany. What I had was a poem cut out of a university newspaper and pinned to the notice board of the Modern Times Book Store. It was written by John Newlove, and Helene told me she had pinned it there, not just because she liked it, but because Newlove was a homegrown poet, born in Regina six years before I was. I copied it into my notebook by hand and took it to Mr. McKay. He misunderstood at first, thought it was something I had written myself, and was tremendously pleased with me. I blushed with embarrassment and stammered that it was something I'd merely copied out, that it was written by somebody named John Newlove. He was still pleased with me. He knew Newlove's work and brought me copies of some more of the poems published a year later in *Grave Sirs*, Newlove's first book. It was in reading Newlove with Mr. McKay that I sensed for the first time that it was not wicked for me to want what's beautiful in life and that I could find it by writing my way to it.

John Newlove died on December 23, 2003, the very day I began my final revisions to this book. I met him only once, and he was not in good shape. Drink was everything to him. A handful of his poems are everything to me that poems in our time and place ought to be. If you still wonder why I have written in a way that resists conventional analysis, the answer is found in a poem of his, "The Double-Headed Snake":

> *Not to lose the feel of the mountains*
> *while still retaining the prairies*
> *is a difficult thing. What's lovely*
> *is whatever makes the adrenalin run;*
> *therefore I count terror and fear among*
> *the greatest beauty. The greatest*
> *beauty is to be alive, forgetting nothing,*
> *although remembrance hurts*
> *like a foolish act, is a foolish act.*

...

As one beauty
cancels another, remembrance
is a foolish act, a double-headed snake
striking in both directions, but I
remember plains and mountains, places
I come from, places I adhere and live in.